AF573913

It has been my pleasure to know Valerie Hill for over fifty years. I was extremely impressed with her teaching of the positive "I Can" curriculum. She is an enthusiastic educator and always takes an assignment to the next level, demonstrating the philosophy of "being the best that you can be." She is a spiritual, caring person who exhibits Christ-like attributes.

Tiffany Snow Madsen,
Resource Specialist (retired) Clovis Unified School District

Valerie and Karlene have produced a practical field guide to mental health! The words of inspiration, questions to the reader and space to record our daily thoughts combine to create an inviting doorway to self care. They know we all need a daily dose of hope and optimism. Responding by filling in blanks is much more inviting than a blank page.

Virginia Morgan Scott, MSW,
co-founder of Family Wellness Associates

A Superintendent's hope when he hires a teacher is for their success in the classroom. Valerie's desire to make a positive difference for every student in her care and to enrich their life earned her California State Continuation Teacher of the Year award! Congratulations on continuing to help others in their life journey with this beautiful journal.

Floyd Buchanan Ed.D., Retired Superintendent of Clovis Unified School District Associate Professor Educational Administration at California State University Fresno

I wholeheartedly indorse this daily life "lift". These daily devotionals will teach and encourage you through your life. I have known Valerie for 30 years. Her words of wisdom target enthusiasm and encourage us with helpful thoughts and a plan of action. This journal will be an invaluable tool to live a more rewarding life style.

Mamie McCullough

I have had the privilege of walking beside Valerie Hill as a friend, teacher and colleague for over thirty years. She is an optimistic person who walks the walk and uses every opportunity and tragedy to learn and support other people. Valerie seeks to provide education, support, empathy and compassion to everyone she meets. She frequently acts as a "bridge" in helping people connect to other people and resources. She lives a self-examined life and finds great support in her spiritual community. She speaks to everyone from her heart and I'm sure this book will be an inspiration and support toward healing for all who choose to use it.

Florence P. Creighton, M.P.H., M.S.W.

Karlene is successful doing God's work whether she is speaking to a larger group, or working on a one-to-one basis because she continues to pursue her own spiritual growth. She uses her talent as an artist, skillfully incorporating creative expression as a process, to facilitate acceptance and renewal. Whether a person were dealing with the loss of a loved one, end of relationship or recovery from consuming addictive issues, she inspires hope, gratitude, and the process of healing.

Michele Kilner, Professor Emeritus,
Child and Family Studies at California State University,
Fresno

Karlene Kay Ryan has committed not only her time, but her heart to The Art of Life Program. For the past 5 years, she has invested her gifts of artistry and compassion into the lives of women cancer survivors. Karlene has helped our survivors navigate through their emotions, allowing them to walk away with not only a love for art, but a sense of purpose in their journey. Karlene's influence is demonstrated through her spiritual faith based leadership and her empathetic compassion as she uses her skills of creativity in her outreach. This journal is another way that I see her expanding her service to the Lord.

Jenelle Higton, Executive Director,
the Art of Life® Cancer Foundation

Karlene Ryan has developed her spiritual gifts and has shared her journey with so many people looking to also find a dynamic spirituality to carry them through the joys and challenges of life! I wholeheartedly endorse Karlene and her spiritual endeavors.

Fr. Michael A. Burchfield, M.Div., JCL, MCL, Pastor, Shrine of Saint Therese, Judicial Vicar, Diocese of Fresno

Others come to you as a blank sheet and an open book, within a short period of time you use your gifts to listen to others and connect with them. Within a short period of time you understand others and are able to help discover their inner light; a discovery process to help them discover themselves and their mission in life. You are able to relate because you have walked where they are walking now and you know how to help them break the chains of bondage and suffering replaced with freedom and joy. Your life and your story inspire us who are walking life's journey: the walk is easier with guides like you to help us move forward.

Daniel K Watson, MA
Registered Representative,
NYLIFE Securities LLC (member FINRA/SIPC)

It is with great pleasure that I am able to endorse this wonderful journal written by my long time friend, teacher and mentor, Valerie Hill. I first met Mrs. Hill in 1985 as a lost teenager when I entered into her classroom. As I look back, she was way ahead of the game with her "Positive Thought for the Day", goal setting, an amazing positive attitude and a heart for encouraging others. Over the years I have spent time with Val, Roland and the kids. No matter where I was in my journey (sober or not) she loved me and always was super encouraging. Today I am sober, saved by grace through Jesus Christ! God has entrusted me with a business, "Hope Café and Catering" where we focus on supporting the outcast, outsourced and overlooked. We teach them a trade, how to feed themselves, their families and the community. I will forever be in debt to the countless hours that Val has spent with me, she loved me when I thought I was unlovable, she trusted me when I wasn't trustworthy and not knowing at the time she showed me how to live like Christ.

Tony Lancaster

TODAY is the
FIRST DAY of the
REST of MY LIFE

DEC. 2020

MERRY CHRISTMAS
CAROL!

HOPE WE CAN GET
THROUGH 2021 WITH
MAKING EACH DAY COUNT
AND THANKFUL FOR OUR
BLESSINGS WE DO HAVE!
HOPE, FAITH, CHARITY!
LOVE FOR OUR SAVIOR,
KNOWING HE IS
THERE FOR US!

LOVE YOU
SISTER!
[illegible]

A DEVOTIONAL JOURNAL

TODAY is the FIRST DAY of the REST of MY LIFE

KARLENE KAY RYAN AND VALERIE HILL

Valerie Hill

Published by Tate Publishing & Enterprises, LLC
127 E. Trade Center Terrace | Mustang, Oklahoma 73064 USA
1.888.361.9473 | www.tatepublishing.com

Tate Publishing is committed to excellence in the publishing industry. The company reflects the philosophy established by the founders, based on Psalm 68:11,
"The Lord gave the word and great was the company of those who published it."

Cover design by Joana Quilantang
Interior design by Joana Quilantang

Published in the United States of America

ISBN: 978-1-63122-731-8
Inspiration / Encouragement
14.05.27

In Gratitude to Vicki Lee Conley

The Lord's Mercy and loving kindness are new every morning.

—Lamentations 3:22–23

Dedication

In loving memory of our sons:
Bradley Lawrence Wayte
Timothy Michael Ryan

Devotional Journal Introduction

How I can go about the devotional:

Each day is a fresh start day… To develop a habit, we encourage daily devotional time.

You make entries every day to make sure that you have a time with God's thoughts for you through the biblical passage. Then, there is a positive thought to get you moving in a positive direction.

If one wishes to do more than one page a day just date the entry and continue. Do not distress over a missed day… pick yourself up, dust your self off and start all over again… continue your quest for the habit of devotion each day.

The 6 most important things to do will keep you focused on your goals for the day and if you do not complete them all you will know exactly where to start the next day. You can always go backwards and remember where you've been in mind, body, and spirit.

"God's Words for Me Today" are interchangeable—meaning, you can use any "message" based on what suits the day's events! Find one that resonates with you and begin your devotional and goal setting time. The journal is very user friendly.

Also, remember there are blank pages in the back titled "Doodles and Doodads" pages to write things you want to remember. Sometimes you can sketch a thought, embellish a passage right in the "Doodles and Doodads" page.

Today ______ / ______ / ______ is the first day of the rest of my life.

A date because the faith journey is one day at a time. It is in the choice to establish a daily devotional that conversion and transformation become a way of life. It becomes a commitment to engage in a definite devotional time—writing in the date makes it real.

Today I am grateful for ______________________.

In gratitude, we move out of self and connect with God and remember that every breath and every moment lived is recognized as a prayer of gratitude in communion with his son, Jesus Christ. In gratitude, the dedication of our purpose to praise him and live for him is made.

Today I will ______________________.

First and foremost, I will renew my purpose of giving praise and glory to God. Today, my will is the will of God, as I place myself in his presence and listen to what is his message for today.

Today my goal is ______________________.

Your goal may be to read and add to this journal every day.

Today, I feel ______________________.

My feelings need to be acknowledged through the act of devotional journaling. The act of writing makes the process of growth appear and makes our prayers truthful communication to our father, God.

Prayer for Today ______________________.

Each day there is a short biblical passage that can be memorized and said often during the day as a mantra.

> Arise! Be radiant! Your light has come. The glory of our God is alive in you, no matter that the darkness seems to hem you round. Let the blind grope toward your brightness; let the weak warm themselves at your joy. Open the eyes of your heart and see! Can you feel them fumbling there in their dark? Can you sense the dryness of their heart? AH! The light of God is in you, the wellspring of love in your soul!
>
> Arise! Shine, for your light has come and the glory of the Lord has risen upon you. Isaiah 60:1

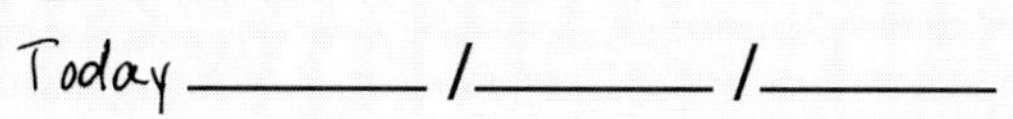

Today ______ /______ /______

God's Words for Me Today: No Worries

Do not fret or have any anxiety about anything, but in every circumstance and in everything, by prayer and petition, with thanksgiving, continue to make your wants known to God.

Philippians 4:6

Today's most important things to do:

1. ______
2. ______
3. ______
4. ______
5. ______
6. ______

I am grateful for ______

______

______

______

Today, my goal is ______

______

______

______

Today, I will ______

______

______

Today, I feel ______

______

Today's Positive Thought

I am designed for accomplishment, engineered for success and endowed with the seeds of greatness!

—Author Unknown

Today ________ /________ /________

God's Words for Me Today: Perfect Peace

You will guard him/her and keep him/her in perfect and constant peace whose mind is stayed on you, because he/she commits himself/herself to you, leans on you, and hopes confidently in you.

Isaiah 26:3

Today's most important things to do:

1. ________________________________
2. ________________________________
3. ________________________________
4. ________________________________
5. ________________________________
6. ________________________________

I am grateful for ________________________________

Today, my goal is ____

____

____

____

Today, I will ____

____

____

Today, I feel ____

____

____

____

Today's Positive Thought

I Can and You Can Too.

—Mamie McCullough

Today _______ /_______ /_______

God's Words for Me Today: His Love

I have loved you, as the Father has loved me; abide in my love.

John 13:9

Today's most important things to do:

1. ______________________________
2. ______________________________
3. ______________________________
4. ______________________________
5. ______________________________
6. ______________________________

I am grateful for ______________________________________

Today, my goal is ______________________________________

Today, I will ______________________________________

Today, I feel ______________________________________

Today's Positive Thought

I'm super good and getting better every day!

—Zig Ziglar

Today ______ / ______ / ______

God's Words for Me Today: His Light

Shine, be radiant with the glory of the Lord for your light has come and the glory of the Lord has risen upon you.

Isaiah 60:1

Today's most important things to do:

1. ______________________________
2. ______________________________
3. ______________________________
4. ______________________________
5. ______________________________
6. ______________________________

I am grateful for ______________________________

____

____

____

Today, my goal is ______________________________

____

____

____

Today, I will ______________________________

____

____

Today, I feel ______________________________

____

____

____

Today's Positive Thought

I'm getting my talents into action for my own satisfaction and the benefit of others.

—Zig Ziglar

Today ________ /________ /________

God's Words for Me Today: Dwell with Him

> Blessed are those who dwell in your house and your presence;
> they will be singing your praises all the day long.
>
> Psalm 84:4

Today's most important things to do:

1. ______________________________
2. ______________________________
3. ______________________________
4. ______________________________
5. ______________________________
6. ______________________________

I am grateful for ______________________________

____

____

____

Today, my goal is ______________________________

____

____

____

Today, I will ______________________________

____

____

Today, I feel ______________________________

____

Today's Positive Thought

Make every day a perfectly positive day!

—Author Unknown

Today ______ /______ /______

God's Words for Me Today: With Wisdom

He who gains wisdom loves his own life; he who keeps understanding shall prosper and find good.

Proverbs 19:8

Today's most important things to do:

1. ______
2. ______
3. ______
4. ______
5. ______
6. ______

I am grateful for ______

Today, my goal is ______

Today, I will

Today, I feel

Today's Positive Thought

Be a meaningful specific.

—Zig Ziglar

Today ______ /______ /______

God's Word for Me Today: Disciple

And He took a cup, and when He had given thanks, He gave it to them saying, Drink of it, all of you.

Matthew 26:27

Today's most important things to do:

1.
2.
3.
4.
5.
6.

I am grateful for ____

____

____

____

Today, my goal is ______________________________________

____

____

____

Today, I will ____

____

____

Today, I feel ____

____

____

____

Today's Positive Thought

You can have everything in life you want if you help enough other people get what they want.

—Zig Ziglar

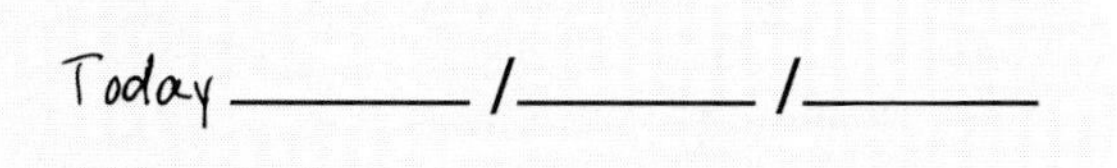

God's Words for Me Today: Joy

I have told you these things, that my joy and delight may be in you, and that your joy and gladness may be of full measure and complete and overflowing.

John 15:11

Today's most important things to do:

1. ______________________________
2. ______________________________
3. ______________________________
4. ______________________________
5. ______________________________
6. ______________________________

I am grateful for ______________________________

____

____

____

Today, my goal is ______________________________

____

____

____

Today, I will ______________________________

____

____

Today, I feel ______________________________

____

____

____

Today's Positive Thought

You are what you are and where you are because of what has gone into your mind. You can change who—what—where you are by changing what goes into your mind.

—Zig Ziglar

Today ______ / ______ / ______

God's Words for Me Today: Friend

I have called you my friends because I have made known to you everything that I have heard from my father.

John 15:15

Today's most important things to do:

1. ______
2. ______
3. ______
4. ______
5. ______
6. ______

I am grateful for ______

______

______

______

Today, my goal is ______

______

______

______

Today, I will ______

______

______

Today, I feel ______

______

Today's Positive Thought

If you always do what you've always done, you will always get what you have always gotten.

—Author Unknown

Today ______ /______ /______

God's Words for Me Today: Your Treasure

For where your treasure is, there will your heart be also.

Luke 12:34

Today's most important things to do:

1. ______
2. ______
3. ______
4. ______
5. ______
6. ______

I am grateful for ______

Today, my goal is ______

____

____

Today, I will ________________________________

____

____

Today, I feel ________________________________

____

____

____

Today's Positive Thought

I can improve who I am and where I am going by thinking, saying and believing positive thoughts.

—Author Unknown

Today _______ / _______ / _______

God's Words for Me Today: His Prosperity

May the Lord bless you out of Zion, and may you see the prosperity of Jerusalem all the days of your life; yes, may you see your children's children.

Psalm 128:5–6

Today's most important things to do:

1. ____________________________
2. ____________________________
3. ____________________________
4. ____________________________
5. ____________________________
6. ____________________________

I am grateful for ____

____

____

____

Today, my goal is ____

____

____

____

Today, I will ____

____

____

Today, I feel ____

____

____

____

Today's Positive Thought

In all aspects of life, you must have a sound foundation on which to build, then you take specific steps to reach life's objectives.

—Zig Ziglar

Today ________ /________ /________

God's Words for Me Today: Sing

Make a joyful noise unto God, all the earth. Sing forth the honor and glory of His name; make His praise glorious.

Psalm 66:1–2

Today's most important things to do:

1. ______________________________
2. ______________________________
3. ______________________________
4. ______________________________
5. ______________________________
6. ______________________________

I am grateful for ______________________________

____

____

____

Today, my goal is ______________________________

____

____

____

Today, I will ______________________________

____

____

Today, I feel ______________________________

____

____

____

Today's Positive Thought

Proper planning prevents poor performance.

—Author Unknown

Today ______ /______ /______

God's Words for Me Today: The Spirit

It is the Spirit of God that made me, and the breath of the Almighty that gives me life.

Job 33:4

Today's most important things to do:

1. ______
2. ______
3. ______
4. ______
5. ______
6. ______

I am grateful for ______

______

______

______

Today, my goal is ______

______

______

______

Today, I will ______

______

______

Today, I feel ______

______

Today's Positive Thought

You pay the price for failure and you enjoy the benefits of success.

—Zig Ziglar

Today ______ /______ /______

God's Words for Me Today: Our Shepherd

I am the Good Shepherd; and I know and recognize my own, and my own know and recognize me.

John 10:14

Today's most important things to do:

1. ______
2. ______
3. ______
4. ______
5. ______
6. ______

I am grateful for ______

Today, my goal is ______

Today, I will

Today, I feel

Today's Positive Thought

Do unto others as you would have them do unto you!

—The Golden Rule

Today ______ / ______ / ______

God's Words for Me Today: The Lord Is My Strength

The Lord is my rock, my firm strength in whom I will trust and take refuge.

Psalm 18:2

Today's most important things to do:

1.
2.
3.
4.
5.
6.

I am grateful for ____

____

____

____

Today, my goal is ____

____

____

____

Today, I will ____

____

____

Today, I feel ____

____

____

____

Today's Positive Thought

Listening is loving.

—Author Unknown

Today ________ /________ /________

God's Words for Me Today: He Has Called Me by Name

I have called you by name: you are mine.

Isaiah 43:1

Today's most important things to do:

1. ____________________
2. ____________________
3. ____________________
4. ____________________
5. ____________________
6. ____________________

I am grateful for ____________________

____

____

____

Today, my goal is ____________________

____

____

____

Today, I will ____________________

____

____

Today, I feel ____________________

____

____

____

Today's Positive Thought

You are somebody! Your ideas count! You were born to win!

—Zig Ziglar

Today ______ /______ /______

God's Words for Me Today: Stay Attentive

All of you must keep awake and watch and pray that you may not come into temptation:

Matthew 26:41

Today's most important things to do:

1. ______
2. ______
3. ______
4. ______
5. ______
6. ______

I am grateful for ______

______

______

______

Today, my goal is ______

______

______

______

Today, I will ______

______

______

Today, I feel ______

______

Today's Positive Thought

Look for the Good in every person in every situation.

—Author Unknown

Today ______ /______ /______

God's Words for Me Today: He Delights in You

The Lord your God is with you, He will take great delight in you, He will quiet you with His Love, He will rejoice over you with singing.

Zephaniah 3:17

Today's most important things to do:

1. ______
2. ______
3. ______
4. ______
5. ______
6. ______

I am grateful for ______

Today, my goal is ______

Today, I will

Today, I feel

Today's Positive Thought

A sincere compliment is one of the most effective motivational methods in existence.

—Author Unknown

Today ______ / ______ / ______

God's Words for Me today: Peace

The Lord make his face shine upon you and be gracious to you; the Lord turn his face toward you and give you peace.

Numbers 6:25–26

Today's most important things to do:

1.
2.
3.
4.
5.
6.

I am grateful for ____

____

____

____

Today, my goal is ____

____

____

____

Today, I will ____

____

____

Today, I feel ____

____

____

____

Today's Positive Thought

People don't care how much you know until they know how much you care.

—Mamie McCullough

Today ______ /______ /______

God's Words for Me Today: In His Favor

Blessed are the people who know the joyful sound; they walk, O Lord, in the light and favor of your countenance.

Psalm 89:15

Today's most important things to do:

1. ______________________________
2. ______________________________
3. ______________________________
4. ______________________________
5. ______________________________
6. ______________________________

I am grateful for ______________________________

____

____

____

Today, my goal is ______________________________

____

____

____

Today, I will ______________________________

____

____

Today, I feel ______________________________

____

____

____

Today's Positive Thought

Many people have gone further than they thought they could because someone else thought they could.

—Zig Ziglar

Today _______ / _______ / _______

God's Words for Me Today: Presence

Let all men know and perceive and recognize your unselfishness. The Lord is near.

Philippians 4:5

Today's most important things to do:

1. ______________________________
2. ______________________________
3. ______________________________
4. ______________________________
5. ______________________________
6. ______________________________

I am grateful for ______________________________

____

____

____

Today, my goal is ______________________________

____

____

____

Today, I will ______________________________

____

____

Today, I feel ______________________________

____

Today's Positive Thought

We can't tailor-make the situations of life, but we can tailor-make the attitude to fit them—before they arise!

—Author Unknown

Today ______ /______ /______

God's Words for Me Today: His Peace

Peace I leave with you; my peace I give you. Do not let your hearts be troubled.

John 14:27

Today's most important things to do:

1. ______
2. ______
3. ______
4. ______
5. ______
6. ______

I am grateful for ______

Today, my goal is ______

Today, I will

Today, I feel

Today's Positive Thought

We do not sing because we are happy, we are happy because we choose to sing.

—Author Unknown

Today ______ /______ /______

God's Words for Me today: Never Alone

I am with you and will watch over you wherever you go.

Genesis 28:15

Today's most important things to do:

1. ______
2. ______
3. ______
4. ______
5. ______
6. ______

I am grateful for ____________________

____

____

____

Today, my goal is ____________________

____

____

____

Today, I will ____________________

____

____

Today, I feel ____________________

____

____

____

Today's Positive Thought

Choose the right. Stay on the Lord's side of the line.

—Author Unknown

Today ________ /________ /________

God's Words for Me Today: His Understanding

Trust in the Lord with all your heart and lean not on your own understanding; in all your ways acknowledge him, and he will make your paths straight.

Proverbs 3:5–6

Today's most important things to do:

1. ____________________
2. ____________________
3. ____________________
4. ____________________
5. ____________________
6. ____________________

I am grateful for ____________________

Today, my goal is ____________________

Today, I will ____________________

Today, I feel ____________________

Today's Positive Thought

People or circumstances cannot make you feel negative—angry—inferior—without your permission.

—Author Unknown

Today ______ / ______ / ______

God's Words for Me Today: His Bounty

I will refresh the weary and satisfy the faint.

Jeremiah 31:25

Today's most important things to do:

1. ______
2. ______
3. ______
4. ______
5. ______
6. ______

I am grateful for ______

______

______

______

Today, my goal is ______

______

______

______

Today, I will ______

______

______

Today, I feel ______

______

Today's Positive Thought

We can improve our lives by improving our attitudes and habits.

—Author Unknown

Today ______ / ______ / ______

God's Words for Me Today: His Care

Cast all your anxiety on him because he cares for you.

1 Peter 5:7

Today's most important things to do:

1. ______
2. ______
3. ______
4. ______
5. ______
6. ______

I am grateful for ______

Today, my goal is ______

Today, I will

Today, I feel

Today's Positive Thought

Never a promise without a plan, know what your six most important things to do today are, do them and have yourself a perfectly positive day!

—Zig Ziglar

Today ______ /______ /______

God's Words for Me Today: His Is the Solution

I am the way, and the truth, and the life.

John 14:6

Today's most important things to do:

1.
2.
3.
4.

5. ______________________________

6. ______________________________

I am grateful for ______________________________

____

____

____

Today, my goal is ______________________________

____

____

____

Today, I will ______________________________

____

____

Today, I feel ______________________________

____

____

____

Today's Positive Thought

Goals are dreams we convert to plans and take action on to fulfill.

—Zig Ziglar

Today ______ / ______ / ______

God's Words for Me Today: Serve the Lord

> Whatever you do, work at it with all your heart, as working for the Lord not for men, since you know that you will receive an inheritance from the Lord as a reward. It is the Lord Christ you are serving.
>
> Colossians 3:23–24

Today's most important things to do:

1. ______
2. ______
3. ______
4. ______
5. ______
6. ______

I am grateful for ______

______

______

______

Today, my goal is ______

______

______

______

Today, I will ______

______

______

Today, I feel ____

____

____

____

Today's Positive Thought

Success occurs when opportunity meets preparation.

—Author Unknown

Today _______ /_______ /_______

God's Words for Me Today: Sing for Joy

Clap your hands, all you people! Shout to God with the voice of triumph and songs of joy!

Psalm 47:1

Today's most important things to do:

1. ______________________________
2. ______________________________
3. ______________________________
4. ______________________________
5. ______________________________
6. ______________________________

I am grateful for ____

____

____

____

Today, my goal is ____

____

Today, I will

Today, I feel

Today's Positive Thought

You, with God's help and personal dedication, are capable of anything you can dream.

—Conrad Hilton

Today ______ /______ /______

God's Words for Me Today: Comfort

Come to me, all you who are weary and burdened, and I will give you rest.

Matthew 11:28

Today's most important things to do:

1. ______
2. ______
3. ______
4. ______
5. ______
6. ______

I am grateful for ____

____

____

____

Today, my goal is ____

____

____

____

Today, I will ____

____

____

Today, I feel ____

____

____

____

Today's Positive Thought

Concentrated thoughts produce desired results.

—Author Unknown

Today ________ /________ /________

God's Words for Me Today: Be Steadfast

Be earnest and steadfast in your prayer, being alert and intent with thanksgiving.

Colossians 4:2

Today's most important things to do:

1. ______________________________

2. ______________________________

3. ______________________________

4. ______________________________

5. ______________________________

6. ______________________________

I am grateful for ______________________________

____

____

____

Today, my goal is ______________________________

____

____

____

Today, I will ______________________________

____

____

Today, I feel ______________________________

____

____

____

Today's Positive Thought

If you want to reach your goal, you must see the reaching in your own mind before you actually arrive at your goal. Be a goal setter.

—Zig Ziglar

Today ______ /______ /______

God's Words for Me Today: Thank You, Jesus

> Give thanks to God on the lyre, sing praises to him with the harp of ten strings, sing to him a new song.
>
> Psalm 33:2–3

Today's most important things to do:

1. ______
2. ______
3. ______
4. ______
5. ______
6. ______

I am grateful for ______

______

______

______

Today, my goal is ______

______

______

______

Today, I will ______

______

______

Today, I feel ______________________________

____

____

____

Today's Positive Thought

Positive thinking and affirmations will not enable you to do anything, but they will enable you to do everything better than negative thinking will.

—Author Unknown

Today ______ /______ /______

God's Words for Me Today: I Have a Friend in Jesus

A friend loves at all times.

Proverbs 17:17

Today's most important things to do:

1. ______________________________
2. ______________________________
3. ______________________________
4. ______________________________
5. ______________________________
6. ______________________________

I am grateful for ______________________________

____

____

____

Today, my goal is ____

____

____

____

Today, I will ____

____

____

Today, I feel ____

____

____

____

Today's Positive Thought

Think it, see it, believe it, expect it and achieve it! Know, be, do and have in the tomorrows of your life.

—Author Unknown

Today ________ /________ /________

God's Words for Me Today: Say the Name of Jesus

Sing to the Lord, O you saints of his, and give thanks at the remembrance of his holy name.

Psalm 30:4

Today's most important things to do:

1. ____
2. ____
3. ____
4. ____

5. ______________________________

6. ______________________________

I am grateful for ______________________________

____

____

____

Today, my goal is ______________________________

____

____

____

Today, I will ______________________________

____

____

____

Today, I feel ______________________________

____

____

____

Today's Positive Thought

Know what you want, say what you want to get what you want in life.

—Author Unknown

Today ______ /______ /______

God's Words for Me Today: I Trust Jesus

For in him does our heart rejoice; because we have trusted in his holy name?

Psalm 33:21

Today's most important things to do:

1. ______________________
2. ______________________
3. ______________________
4. ______________________
5. ______________________
6. ______________________

I am grateful for ______________________

____

____

____

Today, my goal is ______________________

____

____

____

Today, I will ______________________

____

____

Today, I feel ______________________

____

Today's Positive Thought

Decide what you want, decide what you are willing to exchange for it, establish your priorities and go to work.

—H. L. Hun

Today ______ /______ /______

God's Words for Me Today: I Shall Not Want

The Lord is my shepherd; I shall not want.

Psalm 23:1

Today's most important things to do:

1. ______
2. ______
3. ______
4. ______
5. ______
6. ______

I am grateful for ______

Today, my goal is ______

Today, I will

Today, I feel

Today's Positive Thought

A positive family life is vital for the fulfillment and growth of parents and children.

—Author Unknown

Today ____ / ____ / ____

God's Words for Me Today: I Am Never Separate from Jesus

I am with you always, and on every occasion to the close. Amen

Matthew 28:20

Today's most important things to do:

1.
2.
3.
4.
5.
6.

I am grateful for ______________________________

____

____

____

Today, my goal is ______________________________

____

____

____

Today, I will ______________________________

____

____

____

Today, I feel ______________________________

____

____

____

Today's Positive Thought

Family – A tightly knit unit of parents and children forming a household of harmony and beauty.

—Author Unknown

Today ________ /________ /________

God's Words for Me Today: I Am Safe with Jesus

The name of the Lord is a strong tower; the just man runs to it and is safe.

Proverbs 18:10

Today's most important things to do:

1. ______________________________
2. ______________________________
3. ______________________________
4. ______________________________
5. ______________________________
6. ______________________________

I am grateful for ______________________________

____

____

____

Today, my goal is ______________________________

____

____

____

Today, I will ______________________________

____

____

Today, I feel ______________________________

____

____

____

Today's Positive Thought

Learning and knowledge gives us more life, freedom and happiness.

—Author Unknown

Today ______ /______ /______

God's Words for Me Today: I See Jesus in Your Eyes

Live in me, as I do in you.

John 15:4

Today's most important things to do:

1. ________________________________
2. ________________________________
3. ________________________________
4. ________________________________
5. ________________________________
6. ________________________________

I am grateful for ________________________________

____

____

____

Today, my goal is ________________________________

____

____

____

Today, I will ________________________________

____

____

Today, I feel ________________________________

____

Today's Positive Thought

The joy and peace of positive family life, living in harmony and friendship with family members are worth the efforts now.

—Author Unknown

Today ______ /______ /______

God's Words for Me Today: I Am Made Right by His Living in Me

I set the Lord continually before me; because He is at my right hand I shall not be moved.

Psalm 16:8

Today's most important things to do:

1. ______
2. ______
3. ______
4. ______
5. ______
6. ______

I am grateful for ______

Today, my goal is ______________________________

____

____

____

Today, I will ______________________________

____

____

Today, I feel ______________________________

____

____

____

Today's Positive Thought

Be a GOOD finder. Look for the good in every person and every situation.

—Author Unknown

Today ______ /______ /______

God's Words for Me Today: I Have a Song in My Heart for Jesus

Sing to the Lord a new song and his praise from the end of the earth.

Isaiah 42:10

Today's most important things to do:

1. ______________________________
2. ______________________________
3. ______________________________
4. ______________________________

5. ______________________________________

6. ______________________________________

I am grateful for ______________________________________

____

____

____

Today, my goal is ______________________________________

____

____

____

Today, I will ______________________________________

____

____

Today, I feel ______________________________________

____

____

____

Today's Positive Thought

When you don't know how to do something, just start!

—Author Unknown

Today ________ /________ /________

God's Words for Me Today: I Have a Smile on My Face for Jesus

You have said, seek my face—your presence, Lord, will I seek.

Psalm 27:8

Today's most important things to do:

1. ____
2. ____
3. ____
4. ____
5. ____
6. ____

I am grateful for ____

Today, my goal is ____

Today, I will ____

Today, I feel ____

Today's Positive Thought

Making a mistake is no excuse for living as a mistake.

—Mamie McCullough

Today ______ / ______ / ______

God's Words for Me Today: I Am Made in His Image

But it is from Him that you have your life in Christ Jesus.

1 Corinthians 1:30

Today's most important things to do:

1. ______
2. ______
3. ______
4. ______
5. ______
6. ______

I am grateful for ______

______

______

______

Today, my goal is ______

______

______

______

Today, I will ______

______

______

Today, I feel ______

______

Today's Positive Thought

When the student is ready the teacher will appear.

—Author Unknown

Today ______ /______ /______

God's Words for Me Today: Praise His Name

I will rejoice in you and be in high spirits; I will sing praise to your name.

Psalm 9:2

Today's most important things to do:

1. ____________________
2. ____________________
3. ____________________
4. ____________________
5. ____________________
6. ____________________

I am grateful for ____________________

Today, my goal is ____________________

Today, I will

Today, I feel

Today's Positive Thought

Love more, judge less.

—Author Unknown

Today ______ /______ /______

God's Words for Me Today: My Refuge

I will say of the Lord, He is my Refuge and my Fortress my God; on Him I lean and rely, and in Him I trust.

Psalm 9: 9-10

Today's most important things to do:

1. ______
2. ______
3. ______
4. ______
5. ______
6. ______

I am grateful for ____

____

____

____

Today, my goal is ____

____

____

____

Today, I will ____

____

____

Today, I feel ____

____

____

____

Today's Positive Thought

As we see people, we treat them; and as we treat them, often they become.

—Author Unknown

Today ________ /________ /________

God's Words for Me Today: Joyfully Sing

With a solemn sound upon the lyre, for You, O Lord, have made me glad by your works; at the deeds of your hands I joyfully sing.

Psalm 92:34

Today's most important things to do:

1. ____
2. ____
3. ____
4. ____
5. ____
6. ____

I am grateful for ____

Today, my goal is ____

Today, I will ____

Today, I feel ____

Today's Positive Thought

It's not where you start, it's where you finish that counts.

—Author Unknown

Today ______ /______ /______

God's Words for Me Today: Strength

And I will make you to this people a fortified, bronze wall;
they will fight against you, but they will not prevail over you
for I am with you to save and deliver you, says the Lord.

Jeremiah 15:20

Today's most important things to do:

1. ______
2. ______
3. ______
4. ______
5. ______
6. ______

I am grateful for ______

______

______

______

Today, my goal is ______

______

______

______

Today, I will ______

______

______

Today, I feel ____

____

____

____

Today's Positive Thought

Failure is an event, not a person.

—Author Unknown

Today ______ /______ /______

God's Words for Me Today: Be Strong

Be strong and courageous. Do not be terrified; do not be discouraged, for the lord your god will be with you wherever you go.

Joshua 1:9

Today's most important things to do:

1. ________________________________
2. ________________________________
3. ________________________________
4. ________________________________
5. ________________________________
6. ________________________________

I am grateful for ____

____

____

____

Today, my goal is ____

____

____

____

Today, I will ____

____

____

Today, I feel ____

____

____

____

Today's Positive Thought

It's not what happens to you, it's what you make of it that is important.

—Author Unknown

Today ________ /________ /________

God's Words for Me Today: Little Ones

Jesus said: I tell you the truth unless you change and become like little children, you will never enter the kingdom of heaven. Therefore, whoever humbles himself like this child is the greatest in the kingdom of heaven.

Matthew 18:3–4

Today's most important things to do:

1. ______________________________________
2. ______________________________________
3. ______________________________________

4. ______________________________

5. ______________________________

6. ______________________________

I am grateful for ______________________________

____

____

____

Today, my goal is ______________________________

____

____

____

Today, I will ______________________________

____

____

Today, I feel ______________________________

____

____

____

Today's Positive Thought

Be loving and caring.

—Author Unknown

Today ______ / ______ / ______

God's Words for Me Today: In Love

May Christ through your faith dwell in your hearts! May you be rooted deep in love and founded securely on love.

Ephesians 3:17

Today's most important things to do:

1. ______
2. ______
3. ______
4. ______
5. ______
6. ______

I am grateful for ______

______

______

______

Today, my goal is ______

______

______

______

Today, I will ______

______

______

Today, I feel ______

______

Today's Positive Thought

Children are the anchors that hold a mother to life.

—Sophocles

Today ______ /______ /______

God's Words for Me Today: Sing

Speak out to one another in psalms and hymns and spiritual songs, offering praise with voices and making melody with all your heart to the lord.

Ephesians 5:19

Today's most important things to do:

1. ______
2. ______
3. ______
4. ______
5. ______
6. ______

I am grateful for ______

Today, my goal is ______

____

____

Today, I will ____

____

____

Today, I feel ____

____

____

____

Today's Positive Thought

Forgiveness is a gift you give yourself.

—Suzanne Somers

Today ______ / ______ / ______

God's Words for Me Today: King of Eternity

Now to the king of eternity, the only God, be honor and glory forever and ever.

1 Timothy 2:17

Today's most important things to do:

1. ______________________________
2. ______________________________
3. ______________________________
4. ______________________________
5. ______________________________
6. ______________________________

I am grateful for ______________________________________

____

____

____

Today, my goal is ______________________________________

____

____

____

Today, I will ______________________________________

____

____

Today, I feel ______________________________________

____

____

____

Today's Positive Thought

When we hold hands, my fingers smile.

—Beth Mende Conny, about her family

Today ________ /________ /________

God's Words for Me Today: Love Always

Love bears up under anything and everything that comes, is ever ready to believe the best of every person and it endures everything.

1 Corinthians 13:7

Today's most important things to do:

1. ____
2. ____
3. ____
4. ____
5. ____
6. ____

I am grateful for ____

Today, my goal is ____

Today, I will ____

Today, I feel ____

Today's Positive Thought

Faith is the bird that sings when the dawn is still dark.

— Unknown

Today ______ /______ /______

God's Words for Me Today: Love Never Fails

> Love never fails—never fades out or becomes obsolete or comes to an end.
>
> 1 Corinthians 13:8

Today's most important things to do:

1. ____________________
2. ____________________
3. ____________________
4. ____________________
5. ____________________
6. ____________________

I am grateful for ____________________

____

____

____

Today, my goal is ____________________

____

____

____

Today, I will ____________________

____

____

Today, I feel ____________________

____

____

____

Today's Positive Thought

Now and then it's good to pause in our pursuit of happiness and just be happy.

—Guillaume Apollinaire, Italian-born French poet and critic

Today ______ /______ /______

God's Words for Me Today: Father and Son

So that all men may give honor to the Son just as they give honor to the Father, in fact, whoever does not honor the Son does not honor the Father, Who has sent Him.

John 5:23

Today's most important things to do:

1. ______________________________
2. ______________________________
3. ______________________________
4. ______________________________
5. ______________________________
6. ______________________________

I am grateful for ______________________________

____

____

____

Today, my goal is ______________________________

____

____

____

Today, I will ______________________________________

____

____

Today, I feel ______________________________________

____

____

____

Today's Positive Thought

Acting happier than you feel can make you happier than you are.

—Fran Lebowitz, American humorist

Today ________ /________ /________

God's Words for Me Today: Listen

And He arose and rebuked the wind and said to the sea Hush now! Be still! And the wind ceased and there was a great calm.

Mark 4:39

Today's most important things to do:

1. ______________________________
2. ______________________________
3. ______________________________
4. ______________________________
5. ______________________________
6. ______________________________

I am grateful for ______________________________

____

____

____

Today, my goal is ______________________________

____

____

____

Today, I will ______________________________

____

____

Today, I feel ______________________________

____

____

____

Today's Positive Thought

Honesty is the first chapter in the Book of Wisdom. Let it be our endeavor to merit the character of a just nation.

—Thomas Jefferson

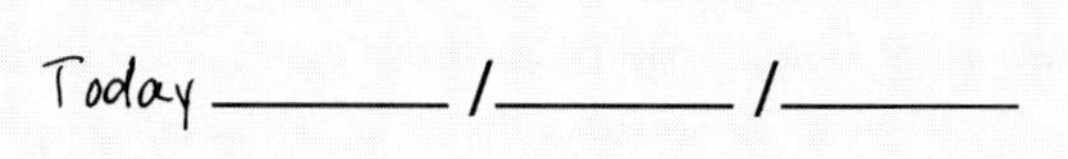

God's Words for Me Today: The Cross

And Jesus, crying out with a loud voice, said, Father, into your hands I commit my spirit! And with these words, He expired.

Luke 23:46

Today's most important things to do:

1. ____________________
2. ____________________
3. ____________________
4. ____________________
5. ____________________
6. ____________________

I am grateful for ____________________

Today, my goal is ____________________

Today, I will ____________________

Today, I feel ____________________

Today's Positive Thought

An honest answer is the sign of true friendship.

—Proverbs 24

Today ______ /______ /______

God's Words for Me Today: Speak Well

> Let no worthless talk come out of your mouth, but only as is good to the spiritual progress of others, that it may be a blessing and give grace.
>
> Ephesians 4:29

Today's most important things to do:

1. ______________________________
2. ______________________________
3. ______________________________
4. ______________________________
5. ______________________________
6. ______________________________

I am grateful for ______________________________

____

____

____

Today, my goal is ______________________________

____

____

____

Today, I will ______________________________

____

____

Today, I feel ____

____

____

____

Today's Positive Thought

My best friend is the one who brings out the best in me.

—Henry Ford

Today ______ / ______ / ______

God's Words for Me Today: Together

For wherever two or three are gathered in my name, there I AM in the midst of them.

Matthew 18:20

Today's most important things to do:

1. ______________________________
2. ______________________________
3. ______________________________
4. ______________________________
5. ______________________________
6. ______________________________

I am grateful for ____

____

____

____

Today, my goal is ______________________________

____

____

____

Today, I will ______________________________

____

____

Today, I feel ______________________________

____

____

____

Today's Positive Thought

Friendship with oneself is all-important because without it one cannot be friends with anyone else in the world.

—Eleanor Roosevelt

Today ______ /______ /______

God's Words for Me Today: He Looks for You

What do you think? If a man has a hundred sheep, and one gets lost, will he not leave the ninety-nine and go in search of the one.

Matthew 18:12

Today's most important things to do:

1. ______________________________
2. ______________________________
3. ______________________________
4. ______________________________

5. ______________________________

6. ______________________________

I am grateful for ______________________________

____

____

____

Today, my goal is ______________________________

____

____

____

Today, I will ______________________________

____

____

Today, I feel ______________________________

____

____

____

Today's Positive Thought

A real friend is one who walks in when the rest of the world walks out.

—Walter Winchell

Today ______ /______ /______

God's Words for Me Today: God Knows Me

> Search me O God, and know my heart! Try me and know my thoughts! And see if there is any wicked or hurtful way in me, and lead me in the way everlasting.
>
> Psalm 139:23–24

Today's most important things to do:

1. ______
2. ______
3. ______
4. ______
5. ______
6. ______

I am grateful for ______

______

______

______

Today, my goal is ______

______

______

______

Today, I will ______

______

______

Today, I feel ____

____

____

____

Today's Positive Thought

Treat people as if they were what they ought to be and you help them to become what they are capable of being.

—Johann Wolfgang von Goethe

Today ________ /________ /________

God's Words for Me Today: For Everyone

I urge that petitions, prayers, intercessions, and thanksgivings be offered on behalf of all men.

1 Timothy 2:1

Today's most important things to do:

1. ______________________________
2. ______________________________
3. ______________________________
4. ______________________________
5. ______________________________
6. ______________________________

I am grateful for ____

____

____

____

Today, my goal is ____

____

____

____

Today, I will ____

____

____

Today, I feel ____

____

____

____

Today's Positive Thought

Happiness is a warm puppy.

—Charles Schultz

Today ______ /______ /______

God's Words for Me Today: Help Me, Oh, Lord

I cry to the Lord with my voice; with my voice to the Lord do I make supplication.

Psalm 142:1

Today's most important things to do:

1. ____________________________
2. ____________________________
3. ____________________________
4. ____________________________

5. ______________________________

6. ______________________________

I am grateful for ______________________________

____

____

____

Today, my goal is ______________________________

____

____

____

Today, I will ______________________________

____

____

Today, I feel ______________________________

____

____

____

Today's Positive Thought

No winter lasts forever; no spring skips it turn.

—Hal Borland

Today ________ /________ /________

God's Words for Me Today: Keep Watch

Therefore, keep watch, because you do not know on what day your Lord will come.

Matthew 24:42

Today's most important things to do:

1. ____

2. ____

3. ____

4. ____

5. ____

6. ____

I am grateful for ____

Today, my goal is ____

Today, I will ____

Today, I feel ____

Today's Positive Thought

Now, God be praised, that to believing souls gives light to darkness, comfort in despair!

—William Shakespeare

Today ______ / ______ / ______

God's Words for Me Today: Ask

You do not have because you do not ask God.

James 4:2

Today's most important things to do:

1. ______________________
2. ______________________
3. ______________________
4. ______________________
5. ______________________
6. ______________________

I am grateful for ______________________

____

____

____

Today, my goal is ______________________

____

____

____

Today, I will ______________________

____

____

Today, I feel ______________________

____

Today's Positive Thought

In all things of nature there is something of marvelous.

—Aristotle

Today ______ /______ /______

God's Words for Me Today: Praise Him

Lift up your hands in holiness and to the sanctuary and bless the lord and gratefully praise him.

Psalm 134:2

Today's most important things to do:

1. ______
2. ______
3. ______
4. ______
5. ______
6. ______

I am grateful for ______

______

______

______

Today, my goal is ______

______

Today, I will

Today, I feel

Today's Positive Thought

A wise man will make more opportunities than he finds.

—Francis Bacon

Today ______ / ______ / ______

God's Words for Me Today: Testimony

God gave us eternal life, and this life is in His Son.

1 John 5:11

Today's most important things to do:

1.
2.
3.
4.
5.
6.

I am grateful for ____

____

____

____

Today, my goal is ____

____

____

____

Today, I will ____

____

____

Today, I feel ____

____

____

____

Today's Positive Thought

Every strike brings me closer to the next home run.

—Babe Ruth

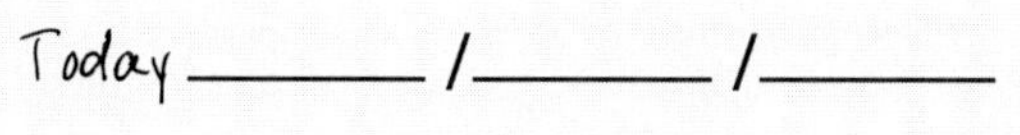

God's Words for Me Today: The Truth

I tell you the truth, my Father will give you whatever you ask in my name.

John 16:23

Today's most important things to do:

1. ______________________________
2. ______________________________
3. ______________________________
4. ______________________________
5. ______________________________
6. ______________________________

I am grateful for ______________________________

____

____

____

Today, my goal is ______________________________

____

____

____

Today, I will ______________________________

____

____

Today, I feel ______________________________

____

____

____

Today's Positive Thought

Genius is eternal patience.

—Michelangelo

Today ______ /______ /______

God's Words for Me Today: Goodness

He has showed you what is good, the Lord requires of you to do justly, and to love kindness and mercy, and to humble yourself and walk humbly with your God.

Micah 6:8

Today's most important things to do:

1. ______
2. ______
3. ______
4. ______
5. ______
6. ______

I am grateful for ______

______

______

______

Today, my goal is ______

______

______

______

Today, I will ______

______

______

Today, I feel ____

____

____

____

Today's Positive Thought

Never think that God's delays are God's denials. Hold on; hold fast; hold out. Patience is genius.

—George-Louis Leclerc du Buffon,
eighteenth century French naturalist

Today ______ / ______ / ______

God's Words for Me Today: Faith

If you have faith like a grain of mustard seed, you can say to this mountain, move from here to yonder place, and it will move; and nothing will be impossible to you.

—Matthew 17:20

Today's most important things to do:

1. ______________________________
2. ______________________________
3. ______________________________
4. ______________________________
5. ______________________________
6. ______________________________

I am grateful for ____

____

Today, my goal is ___

Today, I will ___

Today, I feel ___

Today's Positive Thought

To educate a man in mind and not in morals is to educate a menace to society.

—Theodore Roosevelt

Today ___ /___ /___

God's Words for Me Today: Shine Brightly

Let your light shine before others so that they may see your good works and give glory to your Father who is in heaven.

Matthew 5:16

Today's most important things to do:

1. ___
2. ___
3. ___

4. ______________________________

5. ______________________________

6. ______________________________

I am grateful for ______________________________

____

____

____

Today, my goal is ______________________________

____

____

____

Today, I will ______________________________

____

____

Today, I feel ______________________________

____

____

____

Today's Positive Thought

The essence of all art is to have pleasure in giving pleasure.

—Mikhail Baryshnikov, Russian ballet dancer

Today ______ /______ /______

God's Words for Me Today: Grateful

Give thanks to the Lord, for He is good; for His mercy and loving-kindness endure forever.

Psalm 136:1

Today's most important things to do:

1. ____________________
2. ____________________
3. ____________________
4. ____________________
5. ____________________
6. ____________________

I am grateful for ____________________

____

____

____

Today, my goal is ____________________

____

____

____

Today, I will ____________________

____

____

Today, I feel ____________________

____

Today's Positive Thought

Tell someone that you love and appreciate them today!

—Valerie Hill

Today ______ / ______ / ______

God's Words for Me Today: Holds Your Hand

> Though I walk in the midst of trouble, you will revive me; you will stretch forth Your hand against my enemies, and Your right hand will save me.
>
> Psalm 138:7

Today's most important things to do:

1. ______
2. ______
3. ______
4. ______
5. ______
6. ______

I am grateful for ______

Today, my goal is ______

Today, I will ______________________________

Today, I feel ______________________________

Today's Positive Thought

There is no duty we so much underrate as the duty of being happy. By being happy we sow anonymous benefits upon the world.

—Robert Louis Stevenson

Today ______ / ______ / ______

God's Words for Me Today: Seek

Seek first the kingdom of God and His righteousness, and all these things will be added to you.

Matthew 6:33

Today's most important things to do:

1. ______________________________
2. ______________________________
3. ______________________________
4. ______________________________
5. ______________________________
6. ______________________________

I am grateful for ____

____

____

____

Today, my goal is ____

____

____

____

Today, I will ____

____

____

Today, I feel ____

____

____

____

Today's Positive Thought

Knowing thyself is the height of wisdom.

—Socrates

Today ________ /________ /________

God's Words for Me Today: Holy Spirit

Because you really are his son, God has sent the spirit of his son into our hearts, crying Abba, Father!

Galatians 4:6

Today's most important things to do:

1. ____________________
2. ____________________
3. ____________________
4. ____________________
5. ____________________
6. ____________________

I am grateful for ____________________

Today, my goal is ____________________

Today, I will ____________________

Today, I feel ____________________

Today's Positive Thought

It is only when we truly know and understand that we have a limited time on earth, and that we have no way of knowing when our time is up, that we will begin to live each day to the fullest, as if it was the only one we had.

—Elisabeth Kubler-Ross

Today ______ /______ /______

God's Words for Me Today: Mercy

His mercy and kindness is on those who fear Him with Godly reverence from generation to generation and age to age.

Luke 1:50

Today's most important things to do:

1. ______
2. ______
3. ______
4. ______
5. ______
6. ______

I am grateful for ______

______

______

______

Today, my goal is ______

______

______

______

Today, I will ______

______

______

Today, I feel ______

______

____

____

Today's Positive Thought

Visit a good stationery store and search for a beautiful pen to write within your Today Journal.

—Valerie Hill

Today ______ /______ /______

God's Words for Me Today: Prayer

Our Father who is in heaven, hallowed be Your name, Your kingdom come. Your will be done on earth as it is in heaven.

Luke 11:2

Today's most important things to do:

1. ______________________________
2. ______________________________
3. ______________________________
4. ______________________________
5. ______________________________
6. ______________________________

I am grateful for ______________________________

____

____

____

Today, my goal is ______________________________

____

Today, I will

Today, I feel

Today's Positive Thought

Action conquers fear.

—Pete Zarlenga

Today ______ / ______ / ______

God's Words for Me Today: Holy, Holy

You shall make a plate of pure gold and engrave on it, like the engravings of a signet, holy to the Lord.

Exodus 28:36

Today's most important things to do:

1.
2.
3.
4.
5.
6.

I am grateful for ____________________

____

____

____

Today, my goal is ____________________

____

____

____

Today, I will ____________________

____

____

Today, I feel ____________________

____

____

____

Today's Positive Thought

Do what you can, with what you have, where you are.

—Theodore Roosevelt

Today ______ /______ /______

God's Words for Me Today: Blessed Be His Name

Blessed be the Lord God, the God of Israel, who alone does wondrous things! Blessed be His glorious name forever; let the whole earth be filled with His glory. Amen

Psalm 72:18–19

Today's most important things to do:

1. ____________________

2. ____________________

3. ____________________

4. ____________________

5. ____________________

6. ____________________

I am grateful for ____________________

Today, my goal is ____________________

Today, I will ____________________

Today, I feel ____________________

Today's Positive Thought

It is neither wealth nor splendor, but tranquility and occupation, which give happiness.

—Thomas Jefferson

Today ______ / ______ / ______

God's Words for Me Today: Wait

My soul, wait only upon God and silently submit to Him; for my hope And expectation are from Him.

Psalm 62:5

Today's most important things to do:

1. ______
2. ______
3. ______
4. ______
5. ______
6. ______

I am grateful for ______

______

______

______

Today, my goal is ______

______

______

______

Today, I will ______

______

______

Today, I feel ______

______

Today's Positive Thought

The best way to deal with any problem is to talk it over with three people you can trust absolutely: God, yourself and a friend.

—Author Unknown

Today ______ / ______ / ______

God's Words for Me Today: Listen to Him

Martha, Martha, you are troubled by many things; there is need of only one, Mary has chosen the good portion which shall not be taken away from her.

Luke 10:41–42

Today's most important things to do:

1. ______
2. ______
3. ______
4. ______
5. ______
6. ______

I am grateful for ______

Today, my goal is ______________________________

____

____

____

Today, I will ______________________________

____

____

Today, I feel ______________________________

____

____

____

Today's Positive Thought

Do your best today.

—Valerie Hill

Today ______ /______ /______

God's Words for Me Today: Goodness

Oh how great is your goodness which you have laid up for those who worship you.

Psalm 31:19

Today's most important things to do:

1. ______________________________
2. ______________________________
3. ______________________________
4. ______________________________

5. ______________________________

6. ______________________________

I am grateful for ______________________________

____

____

____

Today, my goal is ______________________________

____

____

____

Today, I will ______________________________

____

____

Today, I feel ______________________________

____

____

____

Today's Positive Thought

Chop your own wood and it will warm you twice.

—Henry Ford

Today ______ / ______ / ______

God's Words for Me Today: Who

Who is the leader of our faith? He, for the joy that was set before Him, endured the cross, despising and ignoring the shame, and is now seated at the right hand of the throne of God.

Hebrews 12:2

Today's most important things to do:

1. ______________________________
2. ______________________________
3. ______________________________
4. ______________________________
5. ______________________________
6. ______________________________

I am grateful for ______________________________

____

____

____

Today, my goal is ______________________________

____

____

____

Today, I will ______________________________

____

____

Today, I feel ______________________________

____

____

____

Today's Positive Thought

"Love yourself first and everything else falls into line, "Lucille Ball advised. "You really have to love yourself to get anything done in this world."

—Author Unknown

Today ______ /______ /______

God's Words for Me Today: Concern

That their hearts may be comforted as they are knit together in love, and that they may become more intimately acquainted with that mystic secret of God, which is Christ, the Anointed One.

Colossians 2:2

Today's most important things to do:

1. ____________________
2. ____________________
3. ____________________
4. ____________________
5. ____________________
6. ____________________

I am grateful for ____________________

____

____

____

Today, my goal is ____________________

____

____

____

Today, I will ____________________

____

____

Today, I feel ______________________________

____

____

____

Today's Positive Thought

Share a positive thought with someone today.

—Valerie Hill

Today ______ /______ /______

God's Words for Me Today: Your Foundation

Have the roots of your being deeply planted and founded in Him, becoming more confirmed and established in faith, just as you were taught, with thanksgiving.

Colossians 2:7

Today's most important things to do:

1. ______________________________
2. ______________________________
3. ______________________________
4. ______________________________
5. ______________________________
6. ______________________________

I am grateful for ______________________________

____

____

____

Today, my goal is ______________________________________

____

____

____

Today, I will ______________________________________

____

____

Today, I feel ______________________________________

____

____

____

Today's Positive Thought

What a wonderful life I've had! I only wish I'd realized it sooner.

—Colette

Today ______ /______ /______

God's Words for Me Today: Be of Sound Mind

For God did not give us a spirit of timidity, but of power and of love and of calm and well-balanced mind and discipline and self-control.

2 Timothy 1:7

Today's most important things to do:

1. ______________________________
2. ______________________________
3. ______________________________

4. ____

5. ____

6. ____

I am grateful for ____

____

____

____

Today, my goal is ____

____

____

____

Today, I will ____

____

____

Today, I feel ____

____

____

____

Today's Positive Thought

Look at the sky at least once a day. Marvel in the majesty.

—Valerie Hill

Today ______ / ______ / ______

God's Words for Me Today: Our Savior

He saved us, not because of any works of righteousness that we had done, but because of His own pity and mercy, by the new birth and renewing of the Holy Spirit.

Titus 2:5

Today's most important things to do:

1. ________________________________
2. ________________________________
3. ________________________________
4. ________________________________
5. ________________________________
6. ________________________________

I am grateful for ________________________________

____

____

____

Today, my goal is ________________________________

____

____

____

Today, I will ________________________________

____

____

Today, I feel ____

____

____

____

Today's Positive Thought

If you aren't fired with enthusiasm, you will be fired with enthusiasm.

—Vince Lombardi

Today ________ /________ /________

God's Words for Me Today: Kindness

Do not forget or neglect to do kindness and good to be generous and distribute and contribute to the needy for such sacrifices are pleasing to God.

Hebrews 13:16

Today's most important things to do:

1. ________________________________
2. ________________________________
3. ________________________________
4. ________________________________
5. ________________________________
6. ________________________________

I am grateful for ____

____

____

____

Today, my goal is ____

____

____

____

Today, I will ____

____

____

Today, I feel ____

____

____

____

Today's Positive Thought

A good marriage is when you're married not to someone you can live with, but to someone you really cannot live without.

—Dr. Howard Hendricks

Today ________ /________ /________

God's Words for Me Today: The Word

We have the prophetic word made firmer still. You will do well to pay attention to it as to a lamp shining in your hearts.

2 Peter 1:19

Today's most important things to do:

1. ______________________________
2. ______________________________
3. ______________________________
4. ______________________________

5. ______________________________

6. ______________________________

I am grateful for ______________________________

____

____

____

Today, my goal is ______________________________

____

____

____

Today, I will ______________________________

____

____

Today, I feel ______________________________

____

____

____

Today's Positive Thought

God is in the details.

—Ludwig Mies van der Rohe

Today ________ /________ /________

God's Words for Me Today: Righteousness

Every Scripture is God breathed for training in righteousness in conformity to God's will in thought, purpose, and action.

2 Timothy 3:16

Today's most important things to do:

1. ________________________________

2. ________________________________

3. ________________________________

4. ________________________________

5. ________________________________

6. ________________________________

I am grateful for ________________________________

Today, my goal is ________________________________

Today, I will ________________________________

Today, I feel ________________________________

Today's Positive Thought

Learn to get in touch with the silence within yourself and know that everything in this life has a purpose.

—Elisabeth Kubler-Ross

Today ______ /______ /______

God's Words for Me Today: He Forgives

If we confess our sins he is faithful and just and will forgive us our sins and purify us from all unrighteousness.

1 John 1:9

Today's most important things to do:

1. ______
2. ______
3. ______
4. ______
5. ______
6. ______

I am grateful for ______

______

______

______

Today, my goal is ______

______

______

______

Today, I will ______

______

______

Today, I feel ______

______

Today's Positive Thought

Treat yourself to a bouquet today.

—Valerie Hill

Today ______ / ______ / ______

God's Words for Me Today: Letting Go

I tell you the truth, unless a kernel of wheat falls to the ground and dies, it remains only a single seed. But if it dies it produces many seeds.

John 12:24

Today's most important things to do:

1. ______
2. ______
3. ______
4. ______
5. ______
6. ______

I am grateful for ______

Today, my goal is ______

____

____

Today, I will ______________________________________

____

____

Today, I feel ______________________________________

____

____

____

Today's Positive Thought

The most important thing about goals is, having one.

—Geoffrey F. Albert

Today ______ /______ /______

God's Words for Me Today: The Lord

The Lord the compassionate and gracious God, slow to anger abounding in love and faithfulness maintaining love to thousands, and forgiving wickedness, rebellion and sin.

Exodus 34:6–7

Today's most important things to do:

1. ______________________________
2. ______________________________
3. ______________________________
4. ______________________________
5. ______________________________
6. ______________________________

I am grateful for ______________________________

____

____

____

Today, my goal is ______________________________

____

____

____

Today, I will ______________________________

____

____

Today, I feel ______________________________

____

____

____

Today's Positive Thought

Anything worth doing is worth doing poorly until you learn to do it well.

—Steve Brown

Today ______ /______ /______

God's Words for Me Today: Pray

But when you pray, go into your room, close the door and pray to your Father, who is unseen. Then your Father; who sees what is done in secret will reward you.

Matthew 6:6

Today's most important things to do:

1. ____________________________
2. ____________________________
3. ____________________________
4. ____________________________
5. ____________________________
6. ____________________________

I am grateful for ____________________________

____

____

____

Today, my goal is ____________________________

____

____

____

Today, I will ____________________________

____

____

Today, I feel ____________________________

____

____

____

Today's Positive Thought

Create a sacred space in your home, a place you can go and quietly read, pray, ponder on things important to you. This place can also be in a garden spot of your yard, created for serenity and beautiful flowers.

—Valerie Hill

Today _______ / _______ / _______

God's Words for Me Today: Serve Him

Being delivered out of the hands of our enemies, we should serve Him without fear, in holiness and righteousness before Him, all our days.

Luke 1:74–75

Today's most important things to do:

1. ______________________________
2. ______________________________
3. ______________________________
4. ______________________________
5. ______________________________
6. ______________________________

I am grateful for ______________________________

____

____

____

Today, my goal is ______________________________

____

____

____

Today, I will ______________________________

____

____

Today, I feel ____________________

____

____

____

Today's Positive Thought

The only difference between successful people and unsuccessful people is extraordinary determination.

—Mary Kay Ash

Today ______ /______ /______

God's Words for Me Today: Glory to the Father

I will do whatever you ask in my name so that the Son may bring glory to the Father.

John 14:13

Today's most important things to do:

1. ____________________
2. ____________________
3. ____________________
4. ____________________
5. ____________________
6. ____________________

I am grateful for ____________________

____

____

____

Today, my goal is ____

____

____

____

Today, I will ____

____

____

Today, I feel ____

____

____

____

Today's Positive Thought

Reputation is what others think about you; character is what God knows about you.

—Adrian Rogers

Today ________ /________ /________

God's Words for Me Today: Be Strong

Be strong and courageous. Do not be terrified; do not be discouraged, for the lord your God will be with you wherever you go.

Joshua 1:9

Today's most important things to do:

1. ______________________________
2. ______________________________
3. ______________________________
4. ______________________________

5. ___________________________________

6. ___________________________________

I am grateful for ___________________________________

____

____

____

Today, my goal is ___________________________________

____

____

____

Today, I will ___________________________________

____

____

Today, I feel ___________________________________

____

____

____

Today's Positive Thought

Each new day is an adventure; an excellent time to make a personal goal.

—Valerie Hill

Today ______ /______ /______

God's Words for Me Today: Little Ones

Jesus said: I tell you the truth unless you change and become like little children, you will never enter the kingdom of heaven. Therefore, whoever humbles himself like this child is the greatest in the kingdom of heaven.

Matthew 18:3–4

Today's most important things to do:

1. ______
2. ______
3. ______
4. ______
5. ______
6. ______

I am grateful for ______

______

______

______

Today, my goal is ______

______

______

______

Today, I will ______

______

______

Today, I feel ______________________

____

____

____

Today's Positive Thought

Write a beautiful letter to yourself. Mail it to yourself. Save it for a day you are discouraged.

—Author Unknown

Today ______ / ______ / ______

God's Words for Me Today: In Love

May Christ through your faith dwell in your hearts! May you be rooted deep in love and founded securely on love.

Ephesians 3:17

Today's most important things to do:

1. ______________________
2. ______________________
3. ______________________
4. ______________________
5. ______________________
6. ______________________

I am grateful for ______________________

____

____

____

Today, my goal is ____

____

____

____

Today, I will ____

____

____

Today, I feel ____

____

____

____

Today's Positive Thought

Anybody can observe the Sabbath but making it holy surely takes the rest of the week.

—Alice Walker

Today ________ /________ /________

God's Words for Me Today: Sing

Speak out to one another in psalms and hymns and spiritual songs, offering praise with voices and making melody with all your heart to the lord.

Ephesians 5:19

Today's most important things to do:

1. ____
2. ____
3. ____
4. ____

5. ______________________________

6. ______________________________

I am grateful for ______________________________

____

____

____

Today, my goal is ______________________________

____

____

____

Today, I will ______________________________

____

____

Today, I feel ______________________________

____

____

____

Today's Positive Thought

"Hope" is the thing with feathers that perches in the soul.

—Emily Dickinson

Today ______ / ______ / ______

God's Words for Me Today: King of Eternity

Now to the king of eternity, the only God, be honor and glory forever and ever. 1 Timothy 2:17

Today's most important things to do:

1. ____
2. ____
3. ____
4. ____
5. ____
6. ____

I am grateful for ____

Today, my goal is ____

Today, I will ____

Today, I feel ____

Today's Positive Thought

It is never too late to be what you might have been.

—George Eliot

Today ______ /______ /______

God's Words for Me Today: Love Always

> Love bears up under anything and everything that comes is ever ready to believe the best of every person and it endures everything.
>
> 1 Corinthians 13:7

Today's most important things to do:

1. ________________________________
2. ________________________________
3. ________________________________
4. ________________________________
5. ________________________________
6. ________________________________

I am grateful for ________________________________

____

____

____

Today, my goal is ________________________________

____

____

____

Today, I will ________________________________

____

____

Today, I feel ____

____

____

____

Today's Positive Thought

If you would lift me up you must be on higher ground.

—Ralph Waldo Emerson

Today ______ /______ /______

God's Words for Me Today: Love Never Fails

Love never fails—never fades out or becomes obsolete or comes to an end.

1 Corinthians 13:8

Today's most important things to do:

1. ______________________________
2. ______________________________
3. ______________________________
4. ______________________________
5. ______________________________
6. ______________________________

I am grateful for ____

____

____

____

Today, my goal is ____

____

____

____

Today, I will ____

____

____

Today, I feel ____

____

____

____

Today's Positive Thought

Commit yourself to finding truth, each day look for spiritual truths.

—Valerie Hill

Today ______ / ______ / ______

God's Words for Me Today: On Eagle's Wings

As an eagle that stirs up her nest that flutters over her young he spread abroad his wings and he took them. He bore them on his wings.

Deuteronomy 32:11

Today's most important things to do:

1. ______________________________
2. ______________________________
3. ______________________________
4. ______________________________

5. ______________________________

6. ______________________________

I am grateful for ______________________________

____

____

____

Today, my goal is ______________________________

____

____

____

Today, I will ______________________________

____

____

Today, I feel ______________________________

____

____

____

Today's Positive Thought

Who am I, where did I come from and where am I going? These are great questions to ponder.

—Valerie Hill

Today ________ /________ /________

God's Words for Me Today: Righteousness

Life is in the way of righteousness and in its pathway there is no death but immortality—eternal life.

Proverbs 12:28

Today's most important things to do:

1. ______________________________________
2. ______________________________________
3. ______________________________________
4. ______________________________________
5. ______________________________________
6. ______________________________________

I am grateful for ______________________________________

Today, my goal is ______________________________________

Today, I will ______________________________________

Today, I feel ______________________________________

Today's Positive Thought

My talents are unique. Only I can be me.

—Valerie Hill

Today ______ /______ /______

God's Words for Me Today: A Time for Everything

> To everything there is a season, and a time for every matter or purpose under heaven.
>
> Ecclesiastes 3:1

Today's most important things to do:

1. ______
2. ______
3. ______
4. ______
5. ______
6. ______

I am grateful for ______

______

______

______

Today, my goal is ______

______

______

______

Today, I will ______

______

______

Today, I feel ______________________________

____

____

____

Today's Positive Thought

Fly your own flag.

—LA Dodgers

Today ______ /______ /______

God's Words for Me Today: Forever

I know that whatever God does, it endures forever; nothing can be added to it or anything taken from it. And God does it so that men will fear Him and worship Him, knowing that HE IS.

Ecclesiastes 3:14

Today's most important things to do:

1. ______________________________
2. ______________________________
3. ______________________________
4. ______________________________
5. ______________________________
6. ______________________________

I am grateful for ______________________________

____

____

____

Today, my goal is ____

____

____

____

Today, I will ____

____

____

Today, I feel ____

____

____

____

Today's Positive Thought

Together we are Giants.

—SF Giants

Today ________ /________ /________

God's Words for Me Today: No Judgment

Do not judge and criticize and condemn others, so that you may not be judged and criticized and condemned yourselves.

Matthew 7:1

Today's most important things to do:

1. ______________________________
2. ______________________________
3. ______________________________
4. ______________________________

5. ______________________________

6. ______________________________

I am grateful for ______________________________

____

____

____

Today, my goal is ______________________________

____

____

____

Today, I will ______________________________

____

____

Today, I feel ______________________________

____

____

____

Today's Positive Thought

Walking 10-30 minutes a day is a perfect time to commune with our Heavenly Father.

—Valerie Hill

Today ______ /______ /______

God's Words for Me Today: Happy Thoughts

> Happy is the man who finds skillful and godly Wisdom, and the man who gets understanding drawing it forth from God's word and life's experiences. For the gaining of it is better than gaining silver and the profit of it better than fine gold.
>
> Proverbs 3:13–14

Today's most important things to do:

1. ______________________________
2. ______________________________
3. ______________________________
4. ______________________________
5. ______________________________
6. ______________________________

I am grateful for ______________________________

____

____

____

Today, my goal is ______________________________

____

____

____

Today, I will ______________________________

____

____

Today, I feel ____

____

____

____

Today's Positive Thought

Smile when you walk.

—Author Unknown

Today ______ / ______ / ______

God's Words for Me Today: The Kingdom

Then the King will say to those at His right hand, Come, you blessed of my Father, inherit the kingdom prepared for you from the foundation of the world.

Matthew 25:34

Today's most important things to do:

1. ______________________________
2. ______________________________
3. ______________________________
4. ______________________________
5. ______________________________
6. ______________________________

I am grateful for ____

____

____

____

Today, my goal is ____

____

____

____

Today, I will ____

____

____

Today, I feel ____

____

____

____

Today's Positive Thought

Sit in silence at least once every day, 10 minutes or more.

—Author Unknown

Today ______ / ______ / ______

God's Words for Me Today: One Another

For when I was hungry and you gave me food, I was thirsty and you gave me something to drink, I was a stranger and you welcomed me.

Matthew 25:35

Today's most important things to do:

1. ______________________________
2. ______________________________
3. ______________________________
4. ______________________________

5. ______________________________

6. ______________________________

I am grateful for ______________________________

____

____

____

Today, my goal is ______________________________

____

____

____

Today, I will ______________________________

____

____

Today, I feel ______________________________

____

____

____

Today's Positive Thought

Listen to good music every day. Classical music is good for your spirit. Hymns are good for your soul.

—Valerie Hill

Today ______ /______ /______

God's Words for Me Today: Chosen Ones

> Clothe yourselves as God's own chosen ones by putting on behavior of mercy, kind feelings, gentle ways patience which has the power to endure.
>
> Colossians 3:12

Today's most important things to do:

1. ________________________________
2. ________________________________
3. ________________________________
4. ________________________________
5. ________________________________
6. ________________________________

I am grateful for ________________________________

____

____

____

Today, my goal is ________________________________

____

____

____

Today, I will ________________________________

____

____

Today, I feel ____________________

____

____

____

Today's Positive Thought

Live with the 3 "E's", Empathy, Energy, and Enthusiasm.

—Author Unknown

Today ______ / ______ / ______

God's Words for Me Today: Be Gracious

Let your speech at all times be gracious so that you may never be at a loss to know how you ought to answer anyone.

Colossians 4:6

Today's most important things to do:

1. ____________________
2. ____________________
3. ____________________
4. ____________________
5. ____________________
6. ____________________

I am grateful for ____________________

____

____

____

Today, my goal is ____

Today, I will ____

Today, I feel ____

Today's Positive Thought

Play more games than last year.

—Author Unknown

Today ______ / ______ / ______

God's Words for Me Today: Give Thanks

O give thanks to the Lord, for his mercy and loving-kindness endure forever.

Psalm 135:3

Today's most important things to do:

1. ____________________
2. ____________________
3. ____________________
4. ____________________

5. ____

6. ____

I am grateful for ____

____

____

____

Today, my goal is ____

____

____

____

Today, I will ____

____

____

Today, I feel ____

____

____

____

Today's Positive Thought

Read more books than last year.

—Author Unknown

Today ________ /________ /________

God's Words for Me Today: Seek Him

I sought the Lord and he heard me and delivered me from all my fears.

Psalm 34:4

Today's most important things to do:

1. ______________________________
2. ______________________________
3. ______________________________
4. ______________________________
5. ______________________________
6. ______________________________

I am grateful for ______________________________

____

____

____

Today, my goal is ______________________________

____

____

____

Today, I will ______________________________

____

____

Today, I feel ______________________________

____

____

____

Today's Positive Thought

Life is like school, we're here to learn.

—Author Unknown

Today _______ / _______ / _______

God's Words for Me Today: The Angel Said

> But our citizenship is in heaven. And we eagerly await a Savior from there, the Lord Jesus Christ, who, by the power that enables him to bring everything under his control, will transform our lowly bodies so that they will be like his glorious body.
>
> Philippians 3:20-21

Today's most important things to do:

1. ______________________________
2. ______________________________
3. ______________________________
4. ______________________________
5. ______________________________
6. ______________________________

I am grateful for ______________________________

____

____

____

Today, my goal is ______________________________

____

____

____

Today, I will ______________________________

____

____

Today, I feel ____

____

____

____

Today's Positive Thought

Trials are like triathlons. They never seem to end.

—Author Unknown

Today ________ /________ /________

God's Words for Me Today: Gifts

Every good gift is from above. It comes down from the Father of all light.

James 1:17

Today's most important things to do:

1. ______________________________
2. ______________________________
3. ______________________________
4. ______________________________
5. ______________________________
6. ______________________________

I am grateful for ____

____

____

____

Today, my goal is ______________________________

____

____

____

Today, I will ______________________________

____

____

Today, I feel ______________________________

____

____

____

Today's Positive Thought

Eat breakfast like a King, lunch like a Prince and dinner like a beggar.

—Author Unknown

Today ______ /______ /______

God's Words for Me Today: Beloved

So, beloved, be eager to be found by him without spot or blemish and at peace, free from fears and moral conflicts.

2 Peter 3:15

Today's most important things to do:

1. ______________________________
2. ______________________________
3. ______________________________
4. ______________________________

5. ______________________________

6. ______________________________

I am grateful for ______________________________

____

____

____

Today, my goal is ______________________________

____

____

____

Today, I will ______________________________

____

____

Today, I feel ______________________________

____

____

____

Today's Positive Thought

I am me. No one else has my DNA. I am one of a kind.

—Valerie Hill

Today ______ /______ /______

God's Words for Me today: Listen to His Voice

> If you diligently hearken to the voice of the Lord and do what is right in his sight, I will put none of the diseases upon you which I brought upon the Egyptians; for I am the Lord who heals you.
>
> Exodus 15:26

Today's most important things to do:

1. ______________________
2. ______________________
3. ______________________
4. ______________________
5. ______________________
6. ______________________

I am grateful for ______________________

____

____

____

Today, my goal is ______________________

____

____

____

Today, I will ______________________

____

____

Today, I feel ____

____

____

____

Today's Positive Thought

Agree to disagree. You don't have to win every argument.

—Author Unknown

Today ______ /______ /______

God's Words for Me Today: He Said

Then said the lord to me, you have seen well, for I am alert and active watching over my word to perform it.

Jeremiah 1:12

Today's most important things to do:

1. ______________________________
2. ______________________________
3. ______________________________
4. ______________________________
5. ______________________________
6. ______________________________

I am grateful for ____

____

____

____

Today, my goal is ________________________________

____

____

____

Today, I will ________________________________

____

____

Today, I feel ________________________________

____

____

____

Today's Positive Thought

Make peace with your past so you won't ruin your present.

—Author Unknown

Today ______ /______ /______

God's Words for Me Today: He Heals

And thus, he fulfilled what was spoken by the prophet Isaiah; he himself took our weaknesses and infirmities and bore away our diseases.

Matthew 8:17

Today's most important things to do:

1. ________________________________
2. ________________________________
3. ________________________________
4. ________________________________

6. ________________________

I am grateful for ________________________

Today, my goal is ________________________

Today, I will ________________________

Today, I feel ________________________

Today's Positive Thought

Eat a fresh fruit today.

—Author Unknown

Today ______ / ______ / ______

God's Words for Me Today: Jesus Answered

Truly I say to you, if you have faith and do not doubt, if you say to this mountain, be taken up and cast into the sea, it will be done.

Matthew 21:21

Today's most important things to do:

1. ______________________________
2. ______________________________
3. ______________________________
4. ______________________________
5. ______________________________
6. ______________________________

I am grateful for ______________________________

____

____

____

Today, my goal is ______________________________

____

____

____

Today, I will ______________________________

____

____

Today, I feel ______________________________

____

____

____

Today's Positive Thought

Think of someone in your life whose company you enjoy.

—Author Unknown

Today ______ /______ /______

God's Words for Me Today: Believe

Whoever says to this mountain, be lifted up and thrown into the sea, and does not doubt at all in his heart, it will be done for him.

Mark 11:23

Today's most important things to do:

1. ______________________
2. ______________________
3. ______________________
4. ______________________
5. ______________________
6. ______________________

I am grateful for ______________________

____

____

____

Today, my goal is ______________________

____

____

____

Today, I will ______________________

____

____

Today, I feel ___

___

___

___

Today's Positive Thought

Try to make 3 people smile today.

—Author Unknown

Today ___ /___ /___

God's Words for Me Today: His Spirit

And if the Spirit of Him Who raised up Jesus from the dead dwells in you, then he who raised up Christ from the dead will restore to life your mortal bodies through his spirit who dwells in you.

Romans 8:11

Today's most important things to do:

1. ___
2. ___
3. ___
4. ___
5. ___
6. ___

I am grateful for ___

___

___

___

Today, my goal is ______________________________

____

____

____

Today, I will ______________________________

____

____

Today, I feel ______________________________

____

____

____

Today's Positive Thought

De-clutter today -car, home, garage, -desk you will feel a sense of accomplishment and enjoy your surroundings more than ever.

—Valerie Hill

Today ______ /______ /______

God's Words for Me Today: Yes

For as many as are the promises of God, they all find their yes in Christ. For this reason we also utter the amen to God through Christ to the glory of God.

2 Corinthians 1:20

Today's most important things to do:

1. ______________________________
2. ______________________________
3. ______________________________

4. ______________________________

5. ______________________________

6. ______________________________

I am grateful for ______________________________

____

____

____

Today, my goal is ______________________________

____

____

____

Today, I will ______________________________

____

____

Today, I feel ______________________________

____

____

____

Today's Positive Thought

No gossiping or regretting the past or negative thoughts.

—Author Unknown

Today ______ /______ /______

God's Words for Me Today: The Angel Said

> The angel said to them, do not be afraid; for behold, I bring you good news of a great joy which will come to all the people. For to you is born a Savior, who is Christ the Lord.
>
> Luke 2:10–11

Today's most important things to do:

1. ______________________________
2. ______________________________
3. ______________________________
4. ______________________________
5. ______________________________
6. ______________________________

I am grateful for ______________________________

____

____

____

Today, my goal is ______________________________

____

____

____

Today, I will ______________________________

____

____

Today, I feel ____________________

____

____

____

Today's Positive Thought

Comparing yourself to others is not a good practice.

—Author Unknown

Today ______ /______ /______

God's Words for Me Today: Gifts

Every good gift is from above. It comes down from the Father of all light.

James 1:17

Today's most important things to do:

1. ____________________
2. ____________________
3. ____________________
4. ____________________
5. ____________________
6. ____________________

I am grateful for ____________________

____

____

____

Today, my goal is ______________________________

____

____

____

Today, I will ______________________________

____

____

Today, I feel ______________________________

____

____

____

Today's Positive Thought

You are in charge of your own happiness.

—Author Unknown

Today ______ /______ /______

God's Words for Me Today: Beloved

So, beloved, be eager to be found by him without spot or blemish and at peace, free from fears and moral conflicts.

2 Peter 3:15

Today's most important things to do:

1. ______________________________
2. ______________________________
3. ______________________________
4. ______________________________

5. ______________________________

6. ______________________________

I am grateful for ______________________________

____

____

____

Today, my goal is ______________________________

____

____

____

Today, I will ______________________________

____

____

Today, I feel ______________________________

____

____

____

Today's Positive Thought

Think about your childhood today. Be grateful for your memories.

—Valerie Hill

Today ______ /______ /______

God's Words for Me Today: Listen to His Voice

If you diligently hearken to the voice of the Lord and do what is right in his sight, I will put none of the diseases upon you which I brought upon the Egyptians; for I am the Lord who heals you.

Exodus 15:26

Today's most important things to do:

1. ______
2. ______
3. ______
4. ______
5. ______
6. ______

I am grateful for ______

______

______

______

Today, my goal is ______

______

______

______

Today, I will ______

______

______

Today, I feel ____

____

____

____

Today's Positive Thought

No matter how good or bad your day is it will change.

—Author Unknown

Today ________ /________ /________

God's Words for Me Today: He Said

Then said the lord to me, you have seen well, for I am alert and active watching over my word to perform it.

Jeremiah 1:12

Today's most important things to do:

1. ________________________________
2. ________________________________
3. ________________________________
4. ________________________________
5. ________________________________
6. ________________________________

I am grateful for ____

____

____

____

Today, my goal is ____

____

____

____

Today, I will ____

____

____

Today, I feel ____

____

____

____

Today's Positive Thought

Stay on good terms with your friends.

—Author Unknown

Today ______ /______ /______

God's Words for Me Today: He Heals

And thus, he fulfilled what was spoken by the prophet Isaiah; he himself took our weaknesses and infirmities and bore away our diseases.

Matthew 8:17

Today's most important things to do:

1. ______________________________
2. ______________________________
3. ______________________________
4. ______________________________

5. ______________________________

6. ______________________________

I am grateful for ______________________________

____

____

____

Today, my goal is ______________________________

____

____

____

Today, I will ______________________________

____

____

Today, I feel ______________________________

____

____

____

Today's Positive Thought

Get rid of everything that's not useful!

—Author Unknown

Today ______ /______ /______

God's Words for Me Today: Jesus Answered

Truly I say to you, if you have faith and do not doubt, if you say to this mountain, be taken up and cast into the sea, it will be done.

—Matthew 21:21

Today's most important things to do:

1. ______________________________

2. ______________________________

3. ______________________________

4. ______________________________

5. ______________________________

6. ______________________________

I am grateful for ______________________________

____

____

____

Today, my goal is ______________________________

____

____

____

Today, I will ______________________________

____

____

Today, I feel ______________________________

____

____

____

Today's Positive Thought

You already have everything you will ever need. Look at the sky at least once a day. Marvel in the majesty.

—Valerie Hill

Today ______ /______ /______

God's Words for Me Today: Good Works

He who began a good work in you will continue until the day of Jesus Christ's return, developing that good work and perfecting and bringing it to full completion in you.

Philippians 1:6

Today's most important things to do:

1. ____________________
2. ____________________
3. ____________________
4. ____________________
5. ____________________
6. ____________________

I am grateful for ____________________

____

____

____

Today, my goal is ____________________

____

____

____

Today, I will ____________________

____

____

Today, I feel ____

____

____

____

Today's Positive Thought

Buy a veggie plant or herb of your choice (tomato, pepper, parsley rosemary, thyme, oregano) nurture and enjoy.

—Valerie Hill

Today ______ /______ /______

God's Words for Me Today: God's Strength

For it is God who is all the while at work in you both to will and to work for his good pleasure and satisfaction and delight.

Philippians 2:13

Today's most important things to do:

1. ______________________________
2. ______________________________
3. ______________________________
4. ______________________________
5. ______________________________
6. ______________________________

I am grateful for ____

____

____

____

Today, my goal is ____

____

____

____

Today, I will ____

____

____

Today, I feel ____

____

____

____

Today's Positive Thought

The best is yet to come.

—Author Unknown

Today ________ /________ /________

God's Words for Me Today: Self-Control

Whatever you do, work at it with all your heart, as working for the Lord, not for men.

Colossians 3:23

Today's most important things to do:

1. ______________________________
2. ______________________________
3. ______________________________
4. ______________________________

5. ______________________________

6. ______________________________

I am grateful for ______________________________

____

____

____

Today, my goal is ______________________________

____

____

____

Today, I will ______________________________

____

____

Today, I feel ______________________________

____

____

____

Today's Positive Thought

In the game of life, before you can get anything out, you must put something in.

—Author Unknown

Today ________ /________ /________

God's Words for Me Today: Hold Fast

Let us hold fast without wavering the hope we cherish for he who promised, is reliable and faithful to his word.

Hebrews 10:23

Today's most important things to do:

1. ______________________________

2. ______________________________

3. ______________________________

4. ______________________________

5. ______________________________

6. ______________________________

I am grateful for ______________________________

____

____

____

Today, my goal is ______________________________

____

____

____

Today, I will ______________________________

____

____

Today, I feel ______________________________

____

____

____

Today's Positive Thought

Send your sister, brother, grandparents or your parents a note; tell them you're thinking about them.

—Author Unknown

Today ______ / ______ / ______

God's Words for Me Today: Pure

But the wisdom from above is first of all pure; then it is peace-loving, courteous, and full of compassion; it is wholehearted and straightforward.

James 3:17

Today's most important things to do:

1. ____________________
2. ____________________
3. ____________________
4. ____________________
5. ____________________
6. ____________________

I am grateful for ____________________

Today, my goal is ____________________

Today, I will ____________________

Today, I feel ______________________________

____

____

____

Today's Positive Thought

Bed time prayers are a great time to thank God for all your blessings.

—Author Unknown

Today ______ / ______ / ______

God's Words for Me Today: Subject to God

So be subject to God. Resist the devil and he will flee from you. Come close to God and he will come close to you.

James 4:7

Today's most important things to do:

1. ______________________________
2. ______________________________
3. ______________________________
4. ______________________________
5. ______________________________
6. ______________________________

I am grateful for ______________________________

____

____

____

Today, my goal is ____

____

____

____

Today, I will ____

____

____

Today, I feel ____

____

____

____

Today's Positive Thought

Think of a success you have had today. Be grateful for the small ones they give you courage to tackle bigger challenges.

—Author Unknown

Today ______ /______ /______

God's Words for Me Today: You Are Healed

He personally bore our sins in His own body on the tree that we might die to sin and live to righteousness. By His wounds you have been healed.

1 Peter 2:24

Today's most important things to do:

1. ______________________________
2. ______________________________
3. ______________________________
4. ______________________________

5. ________________________________

6. ________________________________

I am grateful for ________________________________

____

____

____

Today, my goal is ________________________________

____

____

____

Today, I will ________________________________

____

____

Today, I feel ________________________________

____

____

____

Today's Positive Thought

Do something nice for a neighbor today.

—Author Unknown

Today _______ / _______ / _______

God's Words for Me Today: Beloved

We receive from him whatever we ask, because we obey his orders, follow his plan and practice what is pleasing to him.

1 John 3:22

ay's most in ant things to do:

1. ______________________________

2. ______________________________

3. ______________________________

4. ______________________________

5. ______________________________

6. ______________________________

I am grateful for ______________________________

____

____

____

Today, my goal is ______________________________

____

____

____

Today, I will ______________________________

____

____

Today, I feel ______________________________

____

____

____

Today's Positive Thought

Enjoy life, you only pass this way once.

—Author Unknown

Today ______ /______ /______

God's Words for Me Today: Prosperity

Beloved, I pray that you may prosper in every way and that your body may keep well, even as your soul keeps well and prospers.

3 John 1:2

Today's most important things to do:

1. ______
2. ______
3. ______
4. ______
5. ______
6. ______

I am grateful for ______

______

______

______

Today, my goal is ______

______

______

______

Today, I will ______

______

______

Today, I feel ____

____

____

____

Today's Positive Thought

Inside myself is a place where I live all alone where you renew your springs that never dry up.

—Pearl Buck

Today ________ /________ /________

God's Words for Me Today: Unto Others

And as you would like and desire that men would do to you, do exactly so to them.

Luke 6:31

Today's most important things to do:

1. ____
2. ____
3. ____
4. ____
5. ____
6. ____

I am grateful for ____

____

____

____

Today, my goal is ____

____

____

____

Today, I will ____

____

____

Today, I feel ____

____

____

____

Today's Positive Thought

Undoubtedly, we become what we envisage.

—Claude M. Bristol

Today ______ /______ /______

God's Words for Me Today: Surrender

I appeal to you to make a decisive dedication of your bodies as a living sacrifice, holy and well pleasing to God, which is your service and spiritual worship.

Romans 12:1

Today's most important things to do:

1. ______________________________
2. ______________________________
3. ______________________________
4. ______________________________

5. ______________________________

6. ______________________________

I am grateful for ______________________________

____

____

____

Today, my goal is ______________________________

____

____

____

Today, I will ______________________________

____

____

Today, I feel ______________________________

____

____

____

Today's Positive Thought

Perhaps too much of everything is as bad as too little.

—Edna Ferber

Respect your body. "Know ye not that ye are the temple of God, and that the Spirit of God dwelleth in you?"

—King James Bible of God's Holy Word

Today ______ /______ /______

God's Words for Me Today: Lift Up Your Hands

> Let us examine our ways, and let us return to the Lord. Let us lift up our hearts and our hands up to prayer to God in heaven.
>
> Lamentations 3:40–41

Today's most important things to do:

1. ______
2. ______
3. ______
4. ______
5. ______
6. ______

I am grateful for ______

______

______

______

Today, my goal is ______

______

______

______

Today, I will ______

______

______

Today, I feel ____

____

____

____

Today's Positive Thought

I will tell you what I learned myself. For me a long, five or six mile walk helps. And one must go alone and every day.

—Brenda Ueland

Today ________ /________ /________

God's Words for Me Today: Pray

Confess to one another your faults and pray for one another, that you may be restored to a spiritual tone of mind and heart. The earnest prayer of a righteous man makes tremendous power available.

James 5:16

Today's most important things to do:

1. ____
2. ____
3. ____
4. ____
5. ____
6. ____

I am grateful for ____

____

Today, my goal is

Today, I will

Today, I feel

Today's Positive Thought

The most important opinion is the one you have of yourself, and the most significant things you say all day are those things you say to yourself.

—Author Unknown

Today ____ / ____ / ____

God's Words for Me Today: Humility

Humble yourselves in the presence of the Lord, and he will exalt you. He will lift you up and make your lives significant.

James 4:10

Today's most important things to do:

1. ___________________________
2. ___________________________
3. ___________________________
4. ___________________________
5. ___________________________
6. ___________________________

I am grateful for ___________________________

____

____

____

Today, my goal is ___________________________

____

____

____

Today, I will ___________________________

____

____

Today, I feel ___________________________

____

____

____

Today's Positive Thought

We make a living by what we get, but we make a life by what we give.

—Winston Churchill

Today ______ /______ /______

God's Words for Me Today: One Mind

All of you should be of one and the same mind united in spirit, sympathizing with one another, loving each other as brethren of one household, compassionate and courteous.

1 Peter 3:8

Today's most important things to do:

1. ______
2. ______
3. ______
4. ______
5. ______
6. ______

I am grateful for ______

______

______

______

Today, my goal is ______

______

______

______

Today, I will ______

______

______

Today, I feel ____

____

____

____

Today's Positive Thought

We shall never know all the good that a simple smile can do.

—Mother Teresa

Today ______ /______ /______

God's Words for Me Today: Personal gifts

Each of you has received a gift, a spiritual talent, a gracious divine endowment; employ it for one another as good trustees of God's grace.

1 Peter 4:10

Today's most important things to do:

1. ______________________________
2. ______________________________
3. ______________________________
4. ______________________________
5. ______________________________
6. ______________________________

I am grateful for ____

____

____

____

Today, my goal is ______________________________

____

____

____

Today, I will ______________________________

____

____

Today, I feel ______________________________

____

____

____

Today's Positive Thought

Our words reveal our thoughts; manners mirror our self-esteem; our actions reflect our character; our habits predict the future.

—William Arthur Ward

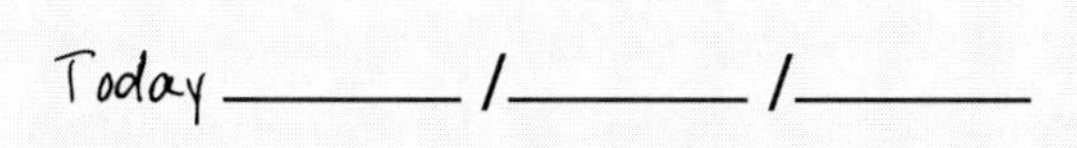

God's Words for Me Today: All Things from Him

For from him and through him and to him are all things. For all things originate with him and come from him; all things live through him and end in him. To him be glory forever. Amen.

Romans 11:36

Today's most important things to do:

1. ________________________________
2. ________________________________
3. ________________________________
4. ________________________________
5. ________________________________
6. ________________________________

I am grateful for ________________________________

Today, my goal is ________________________________

Today, I will ________________________________

Today, I feel ________________________________

Today's Positive Thought

If you judge people, you don't have time to love them.

—Mother Teresa

Today ______ / ______ / ______

God's Words for Me Today: Enter Here

I am the door; anyone who enters in through me will be saved, he will come in and he will go out and will find pasture.

John 10:9

Today's most important things to do:

1. ______
2. ______
3. ______
4. ______
5. ______
6. ______

I am grateful for ______

______

______

______

Today, my goal is ______

______

______

______

Today, I will ______

______

______

Today, I feel ______

______

Today's Positive Thought

It's one of the most beautiful compensations of this life that no man can sincerely try to help another without helping himself.

—Ralph Waldo Emerson

Today ______ / ______ / ______

God's Words for Me Today: My Sheep

The sheep that are my own hear and are listening to my voice; and I know them, and they follow me.

John 10:27

Today's most important things to do:

1. ______
2. ______
3. ______
4. ______
5. ______
6. ______

I am grateful for ______

Today, my goal is ______

Today, I will ______________________________

Today, I feel ______________________________

Today's Positive Thought

God never consults your past to determine your future.

—Mike Murdock

Today ______ / ______ / ______

God's Words for Me Today: Living Bread

I am the living bread that came down from heaven. If anyone eats of this bread, he will live forever, and also the Bread that I shall give for the life of the world is my body.

John 6:51

Today's most important things to do:

1. ______________________________
2. ______________________________
3. ______________________________
4. ______________________________
5. ______________________________
6. ______________________________

I am grateful for ____

____

____

____

Today, my goal is ____

____

____

____

Today, I will ____

____

____

Today, I feel ____

____

____

____

Today's Positive Thought

Love is life—and if you miss love, you miss life.

—Leo Buscaglia

Today ________ /________ /________

God's Words for Me Today: The Truth

And you will know the truth, and the truth will set you free.

John 8:32

Today's most important things to do:

1. ____________________

2. ____________________

3. ____________________

4. ____________________

5. ____________________

6. ____________________

I am grateful for ____________________

Today, my goal is ____________________

Today, I will ____________________

Today, I feel ____________________

Today's Positive Thought

If you have a great ambition, take as big a step as possible in the direction of fulfilling it, but if the step is only a tiny one, don't worry if it is the largest one now possible.

—Mildred McAfee

Today ______ /______ /______

God's Words for Me Today: God Made Man

> God said, Let us make mankind in our image, after our likeness and let them have complete authority over the fish of the sea, the birds of the air, the beasts and over all of the earth.
>
> Genesis 1:26

Today's most important things to do:

1. ________________
2. ________________
3. ________________
4. ________________
5. ________________
6. ________________

I am grateful for ________________

____

____

____

Today, my goal is ________________

____

____

____

Today, I will ________________

____

____

Today, I feel ______________________________

____

____

____

Today's Positive Thought

Make each new morning the opening door to a better day than the one before.

—Author Unknown

Today ______ /______ /______

God's Words for Me Today: Keep His Commands

You shall not add to the word which I command you, neither shall you diminish it, that you may keep the commandments of the lord your God.

Deuteronomy 4:2

Today's most important things to do:

1. ______________________________
2. ______________________________
3. ______________________________
4. ______________________________
5. ______________________________
6. ______________________________

I am grateful for ______________________________

____

Today, my goal is

Today, I will

Today, I feel

Today's Positive Thought

The first wealth is health.

—Ralph Waldo Emerson

Today _____ / _____ / _____

God's Words for Me Today: Blessed

And all nations shall call you happy and blessed, for you shall be a land of delight, says the lord of hosts.

Malachi 3:12

Today's most important things to do:

1.
2.
3.

4. ______________________________

5. ______________________________

6. ______________________________

I am grateful for ______________________________

____

____

____

Today, my goal is ______________________________

____

____

____

Today, I will ______________________________

____

____

Today, I feel ______________________________

____

____

____

Today's Positive Thought

We are not human beings trying to be spiritual. We are spiritual beings trying to be human.

—Jacquelyn Small

Today ______ /______ /______

God's Words for Me Today: Jesus Is My Supplier

Through him all things came into being, and apart from him nothing came to be.

John 1:3

Today's most important things to do:

1. ______
2. ______
3. ______
4. ______
5. ______
6. ______

I am grateful for ______

______

______

______

Today, my goal is ______

______

______

______

Today, I will ______

______

______

Today, I feel ______________________________

____

____

____

Today's Positive Thought

There is a time for everything, and a season for every activity under heaven.

Ecclesiastes 3:1

Today ________ /________ /________

God's Words for Me Today: Jesus Is Faithful

And the father said to him, son, you are always with me and everything I have is yours.

Luke 15:31

Today's most important things to do:

1. ______________________________
2. ______________________________
3. ______________________________
4. ______________________________
5. ______________________________
6. ______________________________

I am grateful for ______________________________

____

____

____

Today, my goal is ____

____

____

____

Today, I will ____

____

____

Today, I feel ____

____

____

____

Today's Positive Thought

Only the heart knows how to find what is precious.

—Fyodor Dostoyevsky

Today _______ /_______ /_______

God's Words for Me Today: Perfect Peace

You will guard him/her and keep him/her in perfect and constant peace whose mind is stayed on you, because he/she commits himself/herself to you, leans on you, and hopes confidently in you.

Isaiah 26:3

Today's most important things to do:

1. ____________________________________
2. ____________________________________
3. ____________________________________
4. ____________________________________

5. ______________________________

6. ______________________________

I am grateful for ______________________________

____

____

____

Today, my goal is ______________________________

____

____

____

Today, I will ______________________________

____

____

Today, I feel ______________________________

____

____

____

Today's Positive Thought

Nothing in the world can take the place of persistence.

—Calvin Coolidge

Today ________ /________ /________

God's Words for Me Today: In Thanksgiving

Let us come before his presence with thanksgiving; let us make a joyful noise to him with songs of praise!

Psalm 95:2

Today's most important things to do:

1. ______________________________

2. ______________________________

3. ______________________________

4. ______________________________

5. ______________________________

6. ______________________________

I am grateful for ______________________________

____

____

____

Today, my goal is ______________________________

____

____

____

Today, I will ______________________________

____

____

Today, I feel ______________________________

____

____

____

Today's Positive Thought

Hands to work, hearts to God.

—Shaker Axiom

Today ______ /______ /______

God's Words for Me Today: Hold His Hand

> Fear not, for I am with you, I am your God, yes, I will help you; yes, I will hold you up with my right hand of rightness and justice.
>
> Isaiah 41:13

Today's most important things to do:

1. ______________________________
2. ______________________________
3. ______________________________
4. ______________________________
5. ______________________________
6. ______________________________

I am grateful for ______________________________

____

____

____

Today, my goal is ______________________________

____

____

____

Today, I will ______________________________

____

____

Today, I feel ____

____

____

____

Today's Positive Thought

Whatever you can do or dream you can, begin it; boldness has genius, power and magic in it.

—Johann Wolfgang von Goethe

Today ______ /______ /______

God's Words for Me Today: His Love

I have loved you, as the father has loved me; abide in my love.

John 13:9

Today's most important things to do:

1. ________________________________
2. ________________________________
3. ________________________________
4. ________________________________
5. ________________________________
6. ________________________________

I am grateful for ____

____

____

____

Today, my goal is ____

____

____

____

Today, I will ____

____

____

Today, I feel ____

____

____

____

Today's Positive Thought

Our perfect companions never have fewer than four feet.

—Colette

Today ______ /______ /______

God's Words for Me Today: His Light

Shine, (be radiant with the glory of the Lord) for your light has come and the glory of the Lord has risen upon you.

Isaiah 60:1

Today's most important things to do:

1. ________________________________
2. ________________________________
3. ________________________________
4. ________________________________

5. ____

6. ____

I am grateful for ____

____

____

____

Today, my goal is ____

____

____

____

Today, I will ____

____

____

Today, I feel ____

____

____

____

Today's Positive Thought

At the end of today I am going to stargaze! I am going look up at the sky, the moon and the stars.

—Valerie Hill

Today ________ /________ /________

God's Words for Me Today: Dwell with Him

Blessed are those who dwell in your house and your presence; they will be singing your praises all the day long.

Psalm 84:4

Today's most important things to do:

1. ______________________________

2. ______________________________

3. ______________________________

4. ______________________________

5. ______________________________

6. ______________________________

I am grateful for ______________________________

____

____

____

Today, my goal is ______________________________

____

____

____

Today, I will ______________________________

____

____

Today, I feel ______________________________

____

____

____

Today's Positive Thought

At the end of today I am going to stargaze again! I am going to surf the beauty of the universe out there in the darkness and light of the moon and stars.

—Valerie Hill

Today ______ /______ /______

God's Words for Me Today: With Wisdom

He who gains wisdom loves his own life; he who understands shall prosper and find good.

Proverbs 19:8

Today's most important things to do:

1. ____________________
2. ____________________
3. ____________________
4. ____________________
5. ____________________
6. ____________________

I am grateful for ____________________

____

____

____

Today, my goal is ____________________

____

____

____

Today, I will ____________________

____

____

Today, I feel ____________________

____

Today's Positive Thought

At the end of this day I am going to stargaze again! I am going to name one of the special stars and make wish.

—Valerie Hill

Today ______ / ______ / ______

God's Words for Me Today: Disciple

And He took a cup, and when he had given thanks, he gave it to them saying, drink of it, all of you.

Matthew 26:27

Today's most important things to do:

1. ______
2. ______
3. ______
4. ______
5. ______
6. ______

I am grateful for ______

Today, my goal is ______

Today, I will

Today, I feel

Today's Positive Thought

Appreciation is the oil that keeps the machinery of human relations working well.

—Mary Kay Ash

Today ______ /______ /______

God's Words for Me Today: Joy

I have told you these things, that my joy and delight may be in you, and that your joy and gladness may be of full measure and complete and overflowing.

John 15:11

Today's most important things to do:

1.
2.
3.
4.
5.
6.

I am grateful for ______________________________

____

____

____

Today, my goal is ______________________________

____

____

____

Today, I will ______________________________

____

____

Today, I feel ______________________________

____

____

____

Today's Positive Thought

Each day comes bearing its own gifts. Untie the ribbons.

—Ruth Ann Schabacker

Today _______ /_______ /_______

God's Words for Me Today: Friend

I have called you my friends because I have made known to you everything that I have heard from my Father.

John 15:15

Today's most important things to do:

1. ______________________________
2. ______________________________
3. ______________________________
4. ______________________________
5. ______________________________
6. ______________________________

I am grateful for ______________________________

____

____

____

Today, my goal is ______________________________

____

____

____

Today, I will ______________________________

____

____

Today, I feel ______________________________

____

____

____

Today's Positive Thought

Do not wish to be anything but what you are, and try to be that perfectly.

—St. Francis de Sales

Today ______ /______ /______

God's Words for Me Today: Your Treasure

For where you treasure is, there will our heart be also.

Luke 12:34

Today's most important things to do:

1. ____________________
2. ____________________
3. ____________________
4. ____________________
5. ____________________
6. ____________________

I am grateful for ____________________

____

____

____

Today, my goal is ____________________

____

____

____

Today, I will ____________________

____

____

Today, I feel ____________________

____

____

____

Today's Positive Thought

Home is the place where we create the future.

—T. Berry Brazelton

Today ______ /______ /______

God's Words for Me Today: His Prosperity

May the Lord bless you out of Zion, and may you see the prosperity of Jerusalem all the days of your life; yes, may you see your children's children.

Psalm 128:5–6

Today's most important things to do:

1. ______________________________
2. ______________________________
3. ______________________________
4. ______________________________
5. ______________________________
6. ______________________________

I am grateful for ______________________________

____

____

____

Today, my goal is ______________________________

____

Today, I will ______________________________

Today, I feel ______________________________

Today's Positive Thought

Grandparents are people who play with children whether they are busy or not.

—Lanie Carter

Today ______ / ______ / ______

God's Words for Me Today: The Lord Is My Strength

The Lord is my rock, my firm strength in whom I will trust and take refuge.

Psalm 18:2

Today's most important things to do:

1. ______________________________
2. ______________________________
3. ______________________________
4. ______________________________

5. ________________________________

6. ________________________________

I am grateful for ________________________________

____

____

____

Today, my goal is ________________________________

____

____

____

Today, I will ________________________________

____

____

Today, I feel ________________________________

____

____

____

Today's Positive Thought

Live each day as if your life had just begun.

—Goethe

Today ______ /______ /______

God's Words for Me Today: He Has Called Me by Name

I have called you by name: you are mine.

Isaiah 43:1

Today's most important things to do:

1. ____________________
2. ____________________
3. ____________________
4. ____________________
5. ____________________
6. ____________________

I am grateful for ____________________

____

____

____

Today, my goal is ____________________

____

____

____

Today, I will ____________________

____

____

Today, I feel ____________________

____

____

____

Today's Positive Thought

Hello, sunshine, you make everyday so much brighter!

—Valerie Hill

Today ______ /______ /______

God's Words for Me Today: Stay Attentive

All of you must keep awake and watch and pray that you may not come into temptation.

Matthew 26:41

Today's most important things to do:

1. ______________________________
2. ______________________________
3. ______________________________
4. ______________________________
5. ______________________________
6. ______________________________

I am grateful for ______________________________

____

____

____

Today, my goal is ______________________________

____

____

____

Today, I will ______________________________

____

____

Today, I feel ______________________________

____

Today's Positive Thought

Gratitude is the fairest blossom which springs from the soul.

—Henry Ward Beecher

Today ______ /______ /______

God's Words for Me Today: He Delights in You

The Lord your God is with you. He will take great delight in you, he will quiet you with his Love, he will rejoice over you with singing.

Zephaniah 3:17

Today's most important things to do:

1. ______
2. ______
3. ______
4. ______
5. ______
6. ______

I am grateful for ______

Today, my goal is ______

Today, I will ______________________________

Today, I feel ______________________________

Today's Positive Thought

The heart that loves is always young, may you be forever young.

—Author Unknown

Today ______ /______ /______

God's Words for Me Today: Peace

The Lord make his face shine upon you and be gracious to you; the Lord turn his face toward you and give you peace.

Numbers 6:25–26

Today's most important things to do:

1. ______________________
2. ______________________
3. ______________________
4. ______________________
5. ______________________
6. ______________________

I am grateful for ____

____

____

____

Today, my goal is ____

____

____

____

Today, I will ____

____

____

Today, I feel ____

____

____

____

Today's Positive Thought

You are wonderful.

—Valerie Hill

Today ______ /______ /______

God's Words for Me Today: In His Favor

Blessed are the people who know the joyful sound; they walk, O Lord, in the light and favor of your countenance.

Psalm 89:15

Today's most important things to do:

1. ______________________________
2. ______________________________
3. ______________________________
4. ______________________________
5. ______________________________
6. ______________________________

I am grateful for ______________________________

____

____

____

Today, my goal is ______________________________

____

____

____

Today, I will ______________________________

____

____

Today, I feel ______________________________

____

____

____

Today's Positive Thought

Today remember the amazing *thinks* you have accomplished.

—Vicki Lee Conley

Then remember the amazing *things* you have accomplished, think before you act.

—Valerie Hill

Today ______ /______ /______

God's Words for Me Today: Presence

Let all men know and perceive and recognize your unselfishness. The Lord is near.

Philippians 4:5

Today's most important things to do:

1. ____________________
2. ____________________
3. ____________________
4. ____________________
5. ____________________
6. ____________________

I am grateful for ____________________

____

____

____

Today, my goal is ____________________

____

____

____

Today, I will ____________________

____

____

Today, I feel ____________________

____

Today's Positive Thought

Today dream a little bit-think of all the wonderful things yet to come into your life.

—Valerie Hill

Today ______ / ______ / ______

God's Words for Me Today: Worthy of praise

Whatever is true is worthy of reverence, whatever is just, pure, lovely and lovable. Whatever is kind and gracious, if there is anything worthy of praise, take account of these things.

Philippians 4:8

Today's most important things to do:

1. ______
2. ______
3. ______
4. ______
5. ______
6. ______

I am grateful for ______

Today, my goal is ______

Today, I will

Today, I feel

Today's Positive Thought

No one else has your warm smile and big heart.

—Author Unknown

Today ______ /______ /______

God's Words for Me Today: Seek God

O God, you are my God, earnestly will I seek you; my inner self thirsts for you my flesh longs and is faint for you, so I have looked upon you in sanctuary to see your power and your glory.

Psalm 63:1–2

Today's most important things to do:

1.
2.
3.
4.
5.
6.

I am grateful for ______________________________

____

____

____

Today, my goal is ______________________________

____

____

____

Today, I will ______________________________

____

____

Today, I feel ______________________________

____

____

____

Today's Positive Thought

I must be willing to give up what I am in order to become what I will be.

—Albert Einstein

Today ______ /______ /______

God's Words for Me Today: His Light Shines

By having the eyes of your heart flooded with light, so that you can know and understand the hope to which he has called you, and how rich is his glorious inheritance.

Ephesians 1:18

Today's most important things to do:

1. ______________________________
2. ______________________________
3. ______________________________
4. ______________________________
5. ______________________________
6. ______________________________

I am grateful for ______________________________

____

____

____

Today, my goal is ______________________________

____

____

____

Today, I will ______________________________

____

____

Today, I feel ______________________________

____

____

____

Today's Positive Thought

Your family is who you are.

—Author Unknown

Today ______ /______ /______

God's Words for Me Today: Precious to Him

> Because you are precious in my sight and honored, and because I love you, I will give men in return for you and peoples in exchange for your life.
>
> Isaiah 43:4

Today's most important things to do:

1. ______
2. ______
3. ______
4. ______
5. ______
6. ______

I am grateful for ______

______

______

______

Today, my goal is ______

______

______

______

Today, I will ______

______

______

Today, I feel ____

____

____

____

Today's Positive Thought

You and your family are precious to Him.

—Valerie Hill

Today ______ /______ /______

God's Words for Me Today: Sing a New Song

O Sing to the Lord a new song; sing to the Lord all the earth. Sing to the Lord, bless his name; show forth his salvation from day to day.

Psalm 96:1–2

Today's most important things to do:

1. ______________________________
2. ______________________________
3. ______________________________
4. ______________________________
5. ______________________________
6. ______________________________

I am grateful for ____

____

____

____

Today, my goal is ____________________

____

____

____

Today, I will ____________________

____

____

Today, I feel ____________________

____

____

____

Today's Positive Thought

There are only two ways to live your life. One is as though nothing is a miracle and the other is as if everything is.

—Albert Einstein

Today ______ /______ /______

God's Words for Me Today: Shadow of His Wings

How precious is your steadfast love, O God! The children of men take refuge and put their trust under the shadow of your wings.

Psalm 36:7

Today's most important things to do:

1. ____________________
2. ____________________
3. ____________________

4. ____________________________________

5. ____________________________________

6. ____________________________________

I am grateful for ____________________________________

Today, my goal is ____________________________________

Today, I will ____________________________________

Today, I feel ____________________________________

Today's Positive Thought

Gratitude is not only the greatest of all virtues but the parent of all others.

—Cicero

Today ______ /______ /______

God's Words for Me Today: Life with Love

For with you is the fountain of life; in your light do we see light, oh continue your loving kindness to those who know you.

Psalm 36:9–10

Today's most important things to do:

1. ____________________
2. ____________________
3. ____________________
4. ____________________
5. ____________________
6. ____________________

I am grateful for ____________________

____

____

____

Today, my goal is ____________________

____

____

____

Today, I will ____________________

____

____

Today, I feel ______________________________

____

____

____

Today's Positive Thought

If you always do what you've always done then you will always be what you've always been.

—Author Unknown

Today ______ / ______ / ______

God's Words for Me Today: His Word

For the Word that God speaks is alive and full of power; it is sharper than any two-edged sword, penetrating to the dividing line of the "breath of life."

Hebrews 4:12

Today's most important things to do:

1. ______________________________
2. ______________________________
3. ______________________________
4. ______________________________
5. ______________________________
6. ______________________________

I am grateful for ______________________________

____

____

____

Today, my goal is ____

____

____

____

Today, I will ____

____

____

Today, I feel ____

____

____

____

Today's Positive Thought

If you always do what you've always done you will always get what you always gotten. Is that what you want?

—Valerie Hill

Today ________ /________ /________

God's Words for Me Today: His Child

But to as many as did receive and welcome him, He gave the authority to become children of God, that is, to those who believe in his name."

John 1:12

Today's most important things to do:

1. ______________________________
2. ______________________________
3. ______________________________
4. ______________________________

5. ______________________________

6. ______________________________

I am grateful for ______________________________

____

____

____

Today, my goal is ______________________________

____

____

____

Today, I will ______________________________

____

____

Today, I feel ______________________________

____

____

____

Today's Positive Thought

If our lips are closed to murmuring then our eyes will be open.

—Neil A. Maxwell

Today ______ /______ /______

God's Words for Me Today: Thank You, Jesus

Give thanks to God on the lyre, sing praises to him with the harp of ten strings, sing to him a new song.

Psalm 33:2–3

Today's most important things to do:

1. ____________________
2. ____________________
3. ____________________
4. ____________________
5. ____________________
6. ____________________

I am grateful for ____________________

____

____

____

Today, my goal is ____________________

____

____

____

Today, I will ____________________

____

____

Today, I feel ____

____

____

____

Today's Positive Thought

Procrastination is the art of keeping up with yesterday.

—Author Unknown

Today ________ /________ /________

God's Words for Me Today: Sing Praises

Sing praises to the Lord, for he has done excellent things; let this be known to all the earth.

Isaiah 12:5

Today's most important things to do:

1. ______________________________
2. ______________________________
3. ______________________________
4. ______________________________
5. ______________________________
6. ______________________________

I am grateful for ____

____

____

____

Today, my goal is ____

____

____

____

Today, I will ____

____

____

Today, I feel ____

____

____

____

Today's Positive Thought

God does not begin by asking us about our ability but only about our availability, and if we then prove our dependability he will increase our capability.

—Neil A. Maxwell

Today ________ /________ /________

God's Words for Me Today: He Blesses You!

The Lord bless you and watch, guard, and keep you.

Numbers 6:24

Today's most important things to do:

1. ____
2. ____
3. ____
4. ____

5. ____________________________________

6. ____________________________________

I am grateful for ____________________________________

____

____

____

Today, my goal is ____________________________________

____

____

____

Today, I will ____________________________________

____

____

Today, I feel ____________________________________

____

____

____

Today's Positive Thought

Service is the rent we pay for living. It is not something to do in your spare time; it is the very purpose of life.

—Marian Wright Eddeman

Today ______ /______ /______

God's Words for Me Today: Grace

For it is by free grace that you are saved and made partakers of Christ's salvation through your faith. It is a gift from God.

Ephesians 2:8

Today's most important things to do:

1. ______
2. ______
3. ______
4. ______
5. ______
6. ______

I am grateful for ______

______

______

______

Today, my goal is ______

______

______

______

Today, I will ______

______

______

Today, I feel ______

______

Today's Positive Thought

No one has learned has learned the meaning of living until he has surrendered his ego to the service of his fellow man.

—Thomas Monson

Today ______ /______ /______

God's Words for Me Today: He Made Us

For we are God's handiwork recreated in Christ Jesus that we may do those good works which God planned for us.

Ephesians 2:10

Today's most important things to do:

1. ______
2. ______
3. ______
4. ______
5. ______
6. ______

I am grateful for ______

Today, my goal is ______

Today, I will

Today, I feel

Today's Positive Thought

The dues of discipleship are high indeed, and how much we can take so often determines how much we can give.

—Neil A. Maxwell

Today ______ /______ /______

God's Words for Me Today: Resurrection

Jesus came and stood among them and said, "Peace to you!" He showed them his hands and his side. And when the disciples say the Lord, they were filled with Joy.

John 20:19–20

Today's most important things to do:

1.
2.
3.
4.
5.
6.

I am grateful for ______________________________

____

____

____

Today, my goal is ______________________________

____

____

____

Today, I will ______________________________

____

____

Today, I feel ______________________________

____

____

____

Today's Positive Thought

The chains of habit are too small to be felt until they are too strong to be broken.

—Samuel Johnson

Today ________ /________ /________

God's Words for Me Today: I Am

And God said to Moses, I am who I am and what I am and I will be what I will be.

Exodus 3:14

Today's most important things to do:

1. ____________________________________
2. ____________________________________
3. ____________________________________
4. ____________________________________
5. ____________________________________
6. ____________________________________

I am grateful for ____________________________________

Today, my goal is ____________________________________

Today, I will ____________________________________

Today, I feel ____________________________________

Today's Positive Thought

Sadness, disappointments, severe challenges are events in life not life itself.

—Richard D. Scott

Today ______ /______ /______

God's Words for Me Today: Christ's Peace

Let the peace from Christ rule in your hearts. And be thankful giving praise to God always.

Colossians 3:15

Today's most important things to do:

1. ____________________
2. ____________________
3. ____________________
4. ____________________
5. ____________________
6. ____________________

I am grateful for ____________________

____

____

____

Today, my goal is ____________________

____

____

____

Today, I will ____________________

____

____

Today, I feel ____________________

____

Today's Positive Thought

No one can make you feel inferior unless you give them permission.

—Author Unknown

Today ______ /______ /______

God's Words for Me Today: He Saves Us

He is able to save for all time and eternity those who come to God through him.

Hebrews 7:25

Today's most important things to do:

1. ______
2. ______
3. ______
4. ______
5. ______
6. ______

I am grateful for ______

Today, my goal is ______

Today, I will

Today, I feel

Today's Positive Thought

There are few things more important in life than knowing your place in mortality and your potential in eternity.

—Dallin H. Oaks

Today ______ / ______ / ______

God's Words for Me Today: He Lights the Way

Your word is a lamp to my feet and a light to my path.

Psalm 119:105

Today's most important things to do:

1.
2.
3.
4.
5.
6.

I am grateful for ___

___

___

___

Today, my goal is ___

___

___

___

Today, I will ___

___

___

Today, I feel ___

___

___

___

Today's Positive Thought

Live as though you are going to die and learn as though you are going to live forever.

—Gandhi

Today ___ / ___ / ___

God's Words for Me Today: He Holds Our Right Hand

I am continually with you; you do hold my right hand. You will guide me with your counsel and afterward receive me to honor.

Psalm 73:23–24

Today's most important things to do:

1. ______________________________

2. ______________________________

3. ______________________________

4. ______________________________

5. ______________________________

6. ______________________________

I am grateful for ______________________________

____

____

____

Today, my goal is ______________________________

____

____

____

Today, I will ______________________________

____

____

Today, I feel ______________________________

____

____

____

Today's Positive Thought

Pain is inevitable but misery is optional.

—Barbara Johnson

Today ______ /______ /______

God's Words for Me Today: Love One Another

> No man has seen God. But if we love one another, God abides in us and his love is brought to completion in us.
>
> 1 John 4:12

Today's most important things to do:

1. ______________________
2. ______________________
3. ______________________
4. ______________________
5. ______________________
6. ______________________

I am grateful for ______________________

____

____

____

Today, my goal is ______________________

____

____

____

Today, I will ______________________

____

____

Today, I feel ______________________

____

Today's Positive Thought

We have a moral obligation to be loyal to the royal within us, to be true to our good names, to bear them with dignity and fidelity.

—Robert L. Millett

Today ______ /______ /______

God's Words for Me Today: Ask

This is the confidence which we have in him that if we ask anything according to his will, he listens to and hears us.

1 John 5:14

Today's most important things to do:

1. ______
2. ______
3. ______
4. ______
5. ______
6. ______

I am grateful for ______

Today, my goal is ______

Today, I will

Today, I feel

Today's Positive Thought

Most people can be adversarial but if you wish to know what a man really is give him power.

—Robert Ingersoll

Today ______ /______ /______

God's Words for Me Today: The Meek

The meek shall inherit the earth and shall delight themselves in the abundance of peace.

Psalm 37:11

Today's most important things to do:

1. ______
2. ______
3. ______
4. ______
5. ______
6. ______

I am grateful for ______________________________

____

____

____

Today, my goal is ______________________________

____

____

____

Today, I will ______________________________

____

____

Today, I feel ______________________________

____

____

____

Today's Positive Thought

Give the world the best you have and the best will come back to you.

—Madeline Bridge

Today ________ /________ /________

God's Words for Me Today: A Prayer

Withhold not your tender mercy from me, O Lord; let your loving kindness and your truth continually preserve me.

Psalm 40:11

Today's most important things to do:

1. ______________________________
2. ______________________________
3. ______________________________
4. ______________________________
5. ______________________________
6. ______________________________

I am grateful for ______________________________

____

____

____

Today, my goal is ______________________________

____

____

____

Today, I will ______________________________

____

____

Today, I feel ______________________________

____

____

____

Today's Positive Thought

Forgiveness is a gift you give yourself.

Suzanne Somers

Today _______ /_______ /_______

God's Words for Me Today: His Name

Therefore, by him let us continually offer the sacrifice of praise to God, that is, the fruit of our lips, giving thanks to his name.

Hebrews 13:15

Today's most important things to do:

1. ________________________________
2. ________________________________
3. ________________________________
4. ________________________________
5. ________________________________
6. ________________________________

I am grateful for ________________________________

____

____

____

Today, my goal is ________________________________

____

____

____

Today, I will ________________________________

____

____

Today, I feel ____

____

____

____

Today's Positive Thought

When we hold hands, my fingers smile.

—Beth Mende Conny, about her family

Today ________ /________ /________

God's Words for Me Today: Children of God

Dear friends, now we are children of God, and what we will be has not yet been made known. But we know that when he appears we shall be like him, for we shall see him as he is.

1 John 3:2

Today's most important things to do:

1. ______________________________
2. ______________________________
3. ______________________________
4. ______________________________
5. ______________________________
6. ______________________________

I am grateful for ____

____

____

____

Today, my goal is ______________________________

____

____

____

Today, I will ______________________________

____

____

Today, I feel ______________________________

____

____

____

Today's Positive Thought

Faith is the bird that sings when the dawn is still dark.

—Author Unknown

Today ______ /______ /______

God's Words for Me Today: Through Him

I can do everything through him who gives me strength.

Philippians 4:13

Today's most important things to do:

1. ______________________________
2. ______________________________
3. ______________________________
4. ______________________________
5. ______________________________
6. ______________________________

I am grateful for ________________________________

____

____

____

Today, my goal is ________________________________

____

____

____

Today, I will ____________________________________

____

____

Today, I feel ____________________________________

____

____

____

Today's Positive Thought

Now and then it's good to pause in our pursuit of happiness and just be happy.

—Guillaume Apollinaire,
Italian-born French poet and critic

Today ______ /______ /______

God's Words for Me Today: Do Not Be Anxious

I tell you, do not be anxious about your life as to what you will eat; or about your body as to what you wear, for life is more than food, and the body more than clothes.

Luke 12:22–23

Today's most important things to do:

1. ______________________________

2. ______________________________

3. ______________________________

4. ______________________________

5. ______________________________

6. ______________________________

I am grateful for ______________________________

____

____

____

Today, my goal is ______________________________

____

____

____

Today, I will ______________________________

____

____

Today, I feel ______________________________

____

____

____

Today's Positive Thought

Acting happier than you feel can make you happier than you are.

—Fran Lebowitz, American humorist

Today ______ /______ /______

God's Words for Me Today: Do Not Fear

> There is no fear in love. But perfect love drives out fear, because fear has to do with punishment. The one who fears is not made perfect in love.
>
> 1 John 4:18

Today's most important things to do:

1. ______________________________
2. ______________________________
3. ______________________________
4. ______________________________
5. ______________________________
6. ______________________________

I am grateful for ______________________________

____

____

____

Today, my goal is ______________________________

____

____

____

Today, I will ______________________________

____

____

Today, I feel ______________________________

____

____

____

Today's Positive Thought

Honesty is the first chapter in the Book of Wisdom. Let it be our endeavor to merit the character of a just nation.

—Thomas Jefferson

Today ______ /______ /______

God's Words for Me Today: Jesus Is

I have told you so, yet you do not believe me. The very works that I do by the power of my Father and in my Father's name bear witness concerning me.

John 10:25

Today's most important things to do:

1. ______________________________
2. ______________________________
3. ______________________________
4. ______________________________
5. ______________________________
6. ______________________________

I am grateful for ______________________________

____

____

____

Today, my goal is ____

____

____

____

Today, I will ____

____

____

Today, I feel ____

____

____

____

Today's Positive Thought

An honest answer is the sign of true friendship.

Proverbs 24:25

Today ______ / ______ / ______

God's Words for Me Today: Grace

My grace is enough for you; for my strength and power are made perfect and show themselves most effective in your weakness.

2 Corinthians 12:9

Today's most important things to do:

1. ________________________________
2. ________________________________
3. ________________________________
4. ________________________________

5. ________________________________

6. ________________________________

I am grateful for ________________________________

____

____

____

Today, my goal is ________________________________

____

____

____

Today, I will ________________________________

____

____

Today, I feel ________________________________

____

____

____

Today's Positive Thought

My best friend is the one who brings out the best in me.

—Henry Ford

Today ______ /______ /______

God's Words for Me Today: The Message

> Then does he who supplies you with his marvelous Holy Spirit and works powerfully and miraculously among you, do so on what the law demands, or of your believing in and trusting in and relying on the message that you heard?
>
> Galatians 3:5

Today's most important things to do:

1. ______
2. ______
3. ______
4. ______
5. ______
6. ______

I am grateful for ______

______

______

______

Today, my goal is ______

______

______

______

Today, I will ______

______

______

Today, I feel ______________________________

____

____

____

Today's Positive Thought

Friendship with oneself is all-important because without it one cannot be friends with anyone else in the world.

—Eleanor Roosevelt

Today ______ / ______ / ______

God's Words for Me Today: Each Other

Let each of you esteem and look upon and be concerned for not only his own interests but also for the interests of others.

Philippians 2:4

Today's most important things to do:

1. ______________________
2. ______________________
3. ______________________
4. ______________________
5. ______________________
6. ______________________

I am grateful for ______________________________

____

____

____

Today, my goal is ____

____

____

____

Today, I will ____

____

____

Today, I feel ____

____

____

____

Today's Positive Thought

A real friend is one who walks in when the rest of the world walks out.

—Walter Winchell

Today ________ /________ /________

God's Words for Me Today: Attitude

Let this same attitude and purpose and humble mind be in you which was in Jesus Christ.

Philippians 2:5

Today's most important things to do:

1. ______________________________
2. ______________________________
3. ______________________________
4. ______________________________

5. ______________________________

6. ______________________________

I am grateful for ______________________________

____

____

____

Today, my goal is ______________________________

____

____

____

Today, I will ______________________________

____

____

Today, I feel ______________________________

____

____

____

Today's Positive Thought

Treat people as if they were what they ought to be and you help them to become what they are capable of being.

—Johann Wolfgang von Goethe

Today ________ /________ /________

God's Words for Me Today: Discipleship

Jesus said, if you abide in my word, you are truly my disciples.

John 8:31

Today's most important things to do:

1. ______________________________
2. ______________________________
3. ______________________________
4. ______________________________
5. ______________________________
6. ______________________________

I am grateful for ______________________________

____

____

____

Today, my goal is ______________________________

____

____

____

Today, I will ______________________________

____

____

Today, I feel ______________________________

____

____

____

Today's Positive Thought

Happiness is a warm puppy.

—Charles Schultz

Today ______ /______ /______

God's Words for Me Today: Holy Spirit

When he, the Spirit of Truth comes, he will guide you into all the Truth. He will tell whatever he hears from the Father.

John 16:13

Today's most important things to do:

1. ______
2. ______
3. ______
4. ______
5. ______
6. ______

I am grateful for ______

______

______

______

Today, my goal is ______

______

______

______

Today, I will ______

______

______

Today, I feel ______

______

Today's Positive Thought

No winter lasts forever; no spring skips its turn.

—Hal Borland

Today ______ /______ /______

God's Words for Me Today: Eucharist

And he took a cup, and when he had given thanks, he said, take this and divide and distribute it among yourselves.

Luke 22:17

Today's most important things to do:

1. ______
2. ______
3. ______
4. ______
5. ______
6. ______

I am grateful for ______

Today, my goal is ______

Today, I will

Today, I feel

Today's Positive Thought

Now, God be praised, that to believing souls gives light to darkness, comfort in despair!

—William Shakespeare

Today ______ / ______ / ______

God's Words for Me Today: Holy Eucharist

He took a loaf of bread and when he had given thanks, he broke it and gave it to them saying, this is my body which is given for you. Do this in remembrance of me.

Luke 22:19

Today's most important things to do:

1.
2.
3.
4.
5.
6.

I am grateful for ____

____

____

____

Today, my goal is ____

____

____

____

Today, I will ____

____

____

Today, I feel ____

____

____

____

Today's Positive Thought

A wise man will make more opportunities than he finds.

—Francis Bacon

Today ________ /________ /________

God's Words for Me Today: The Kingdom

My Father has appointed a kingdom and conferred it on me, so I confer on you. That you may eat and drink at my table in my kingdom.

Luke 22:29–30

Today's most important things to do:

1. ______________________________
2. ______________________________
3. ______________________________
4. ______________________________
5. ______________________________
6. ______________________________

I am grateful for ______________________________

____

____

____

Today, my goal is ______________________________

____

____

____

Today, I will ______________________________

____

____

Today, I feel ______________________________

____

____

____

Today's Positive Thought

In all things of nature there is something of marvelous.

—Aristotle

Today ______ /______ /______

God's Words for Me Today: Acknowledge Him

> Everyone who acknowledges me before men, I will also acknowledge him before my Father who is in heaven.
>
> Matthew 10:32

Today's most important things to do:

1. ______________________________
2. ______________________________
3. ______________________________
4. ______________________________
5. ______________________________
6. ______________________________

I am grateful for ______________________________

____

____

____

Today, my goal is ______________________________

____

____

____

Today, I will ______________________________

____

____

Today, I feel ______________________________

____

Today's Positive Thought

Difficulties strengthen the mind, as labor does the body.

—Seneca

Today ______ /______ /______

God's Words for Me Today: An earnest prayer

Hannah prayed, and said, my heart exults and triumphs in the Lord; my strength is lifted up in the Lord. My mouth is no longer silent, for it is opened wide over my enemies, because I rejoice in your salvation.

1 Samuel 2:1

Today's most important things to do:

1. ______
2. ______
3. ______
4. ______
5. ______
6. ______

I am grateful for ______

Today, my goal is ____________________

____

____

____

Today, I will ____________________

____

____

Today, I feel ____________________

____

____

____

Today's Positive Thought

Every strike brings me closer to the next home run.

—Babe Ruth

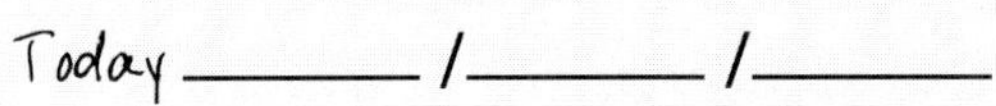

God's Words for Me Today: Keep His Commandments

Take diligent heed to do the commandment and the law which Moses the servant of the Lord charged you; to love the Lord your God and to walk in all his ways and to keep his commandments and to cling to and unite with him and to serve him with all your heart and soul.

Joshua 22:5

Today's most important things to do:

1. ______________________________
2. ______________________________
3. ______________________________
4. ______________________________
5. ______________________________
6. ______________________________

I am grateful for ______________________________

____

____

____

Today, my goal is ______________________________

____

____

____

Today, I will ______________________________

____

____

Today, I feel ______________________________

____

____

____

Today's Positive Thought

Genius is eternal patience.

—Michelangelo

Today ______ /______ /______

God's Words for Me Today: Sacred Place

There shall be a place which the Lord your God shall choose to cause his name and his presence to dwell there; to it you shall bring all that I command you, your choicest offerings which you vow to the Lord.

Deuteronomy 12:11

Today's most important things to do:

1. ______
2. ______
3. ______
4. ______
5. ______
6. ______

I am grateful for ______

______

______

______

Today, my goal is ______

______

______

______

Today, I will ______

______

______

Today, I feel ____

____

____

____

Today's Positive Thought

Never think that God's delays are God's denials. Hold on; hold fast; hold out. Patience is genius.

—George-Louis Leclerc du Buffon,
eighteenth-century French naturalist

Today ______ /______ /______

God's Words for Me Today: A Covenant

Then God spoke to Noah and to his sons with him, saying, Behold, I establish my covenant with you and with your descendants after you.

Genesis 9:8–9

Today's most important things to do:

1. ______________________________
2. ______________________________
3. ______________________________
4. ______________________________
5. ______________________________
6. ______________________________

I am grateful for ____

____

Today, my goal is

Today, I will

Today, I feel

Today's Positive Thought

To educate a man in mind and not in morals is to educate a menace to society.

—Theodore Roosevelt

Today ______ /______ /______

God's Words for Me Today: First Couple

Adam said this creature is now bone of my bones and flesh of my flesh; she shall be called woman, because she was taken out of a man.

Genesis 2:23

Today's most important things to do:

1. ____________________
2. ____________________
3. ____________________
4. ____________________
5. ____________________
6. ____________________

I am grateful for ____________________

Today, my goal is ____________________

Today, I will ____________________

Today, I feel ____________________

Today's Positive Thought

The essence of all art is to have pleasure in giving pleasure.

—Mikhail Baryshnikov, Russian ballet dancer

Today ______ /______ /______

God's Words for Me Today: From the Heart

All the ways of a man are pure in his own eyes, but the Lord weighs the spirits of the heart. Roll your works upon the Lord and trust them to him; he will cause your thoughts to become agreeable to his will, and so shall your plans be established and succeed.

Proverbs 16:2–3

Today's most important things to do:

1. ____________________
2. ____________________
3. ____________________
4. ____________________
5. ____________________
6. ____________________

I am grateful for ____________________

____

____

____

Today, my goal is ____________________

____

____

____

Today, I will ____________________

____

____

Today, I feel ____

____

____

____

Today's Positive Thought

God-made object like a tree or flower. If it clashes, it is not art.

—Marc Chagall

Today ______ /______ /______

God's Words for Me Today: Wisdom

For the Lord gives skillful and godly wisdom; from his mouth come knowledge and understanding.

Proverbs 2:6

Today's most important things to do:

1. ________________________________
2. ________________________________
3. ________________________________
4. ________________________________
5. ________________________________
6. ________________________________

I am grateful for ____

____

____

____

Today, my goal is ______________________________

____

____

____

Today, I will ______________________________

____

____

Today, I feel ______________________________

____

____

____

Today's Positive Thought

I have no special talent. I am only passionately curious.

—Albert Einstein

Today ______ / ______ / ______

God's Words for Me Today: Listen Carefully

Hear, o my son, and receive my sayings, and the years of your life shall be many. I have taught you in the way of skillful wisdom; I have led you in paths of uprightness.

Proverbs 4:10–11

Today's most important things to do:

1. ______________________________
2. ______________________________
3. ______________________________
4. ______________________________

5. ______________________________

6. ______________________________

I am grateful for ______________________________

____

____

____

Today, my goal is ______________________________

____

____

____

Today, I will ______________________________

____

____

Today, I feel ______________________________

____

____

____

Today's Positive Thought

Discouragement and failure are two of the surest stepping stones to success. Develop success from failures.

—Dale Carnegie

Today ______ /______ /______

God's Words for Me Today: A Prize

> Prize wisdom highly and exalt her, and she will exalt and promote you, she shall give to your head a wreath of gracefulness; a crown of beauty and glory will she deliver to you.
>
> Proverbs 4:8–9

Today's most important things to do:

1. ______
2. ______
3. ______
4. ______
5. ______
6. ______

I am grateful for ______

______

______

______

Today, my goal is ______

______

______

______

Today, I will ______

______

______

Today, I feel ____

____

____

____

Today's Positive Thought

Kindness matters.

—Author Unknown

Today ______ /______ /______

God's Words for Me Today: Standing Firm

It is God who confirms and makes us steadfast and establishes us with you in Christ, and has consecrated and anointed us with the gifts of the Holy Spirit.

2 Corinthians 1:21

Today's most important things to do:

1. ______________________________
2. ______________________________
3. ______________________________
4. ______________________________
5. ______________________________
6. ______________________________

I am grateful for ____

____

____

____

Today, my goal is ____

____

____

____

Today, I will ____

____

____

Today, I feel ____

____

____

____

Today's Positive Thought

Attitudes are contagious. Is yours worth catching?

—Author Unknown

Today ______ /______ /______

God's Words for Me Today: Always with Us

For though the mountains should depart and the hills be shaken, yet my love and kindness shall not depart from you, nor my covenant of peace and completeness be removed.

Isaiah 54:10

Today's most important things to do:

1. ______________________________
2. ______________________________
3. ______________________________
4. ______________________________

5. ____

6. ____

I am grateful for ____

____

____

____

Today, my goal is ____

____

____

____

Today, I will ____

____

____

Today, I feel ____

____

____

____

Today's Positive Thought

True love stories never have endings.

—Richard Bach

Today ______ /______ /______

God's Words for Me Today: Rejoice in the Lord

I will greatly rejoice in the lord, my soul will exult in my God; for he has clothed me with the garments of salvation.

Isaiah 61:10

Today's most important things to do:

1. ______
2. ______
3. ______
4. ______
5. ______
6. ______

I am grateful for ______

______

______

______

Today, my goal is ______

______

______

______

Today, I will ______

______

______

Today, I feel ____

____

____

____

Today's Positive Thought

Just when the caterpillar thought the world was over, it became a butterfly.

—Proverbs, The Holy Bible

Today ______ / ______ / ______

God's Words for Me Today: Love the Lord

I love the Lord, because he has heard my voice and my supplications. Because he has inclined his ear to me, therefore will I call upon him as long as I live.

Psalm 116:1–2

Today's most important things to do:

1. ______________________________
2. ______________________________
3. ______________________________
4. ______________________________
5. ______________________________
6. ______________________________

I am grateful for ____

____

____

____

Today, my goal is ______________________________

____

____

____

Today, I will ______________________________

____

____

Today, I feel ______________________________

____

____

____

Today's Positive Thought

Take the first step in faith. You don't have to see the whole staircase, just take the first step.

—Martin Luther King Jr.

Today ______ /______ /______

God's Words for Me Today: In Spirit

For though I am away from you in body, yet I am with you in spirit, delighted at the sight of your steadfastness of your faith in Christ.

Colossians 2:5

Today's most important things to do:

1. ______________________________
2. ______________________________
3. ______________________________
4. ______________________________

5. ______________________________

6. ______________________________

I am grateful for ______________________________

____

____

____

Today, my goal is ______________________________

____

____

____

Today, I will ______________________________

____

____

Today, I feel ______________________________

____

____

____

Today's Positive Thought

Friendship isn't about whom you have known the longest. It's about who came, and never left your side.

—Author unknown

Today ______ / ______ / ______

God's Words for Me Today: In His Name

> And whatever you do in word or deed, do everything in the name of the Lord Jesus and giving praise to God the father through him.
>
> Colossians 3:17

Today's most important things to do:

1. ______________________________
2. ______________________________
3. ______________________________
4. ______________________________
5. ______________________________
6. ______________________________

I am grateful for ______________________________

____

____

____

Today, my goal is ______________________________

____

____

____

Today, I will ______________________________

____

____

Today, I feel ______________________________

____

____

____

Today's Positive Thought

Your imagination is your preview of life's coming attractions.

—Albert Einstein

Today ______ /______ /______

God's Words for Me Today: Peace to You

Now may the Lord of peace Himself grant you His peace at all times and in all ways. The Lord be with you.

2 Thessalonians 3:16

Today's most important things to do:

1. ______________________________
2. ______________________________
3. ______________________________
4. ______________________________
5. ______________________________
6. ______________________________

I am grateful for ______________________________

____

____

____

Today, my goal is ______________________________

____

____

____

Today, I will ______________________________

____

____

Today, I feel ______________________________

____

____

____

Today's Positive Thought

A hundred years from now, it will not matter what my bank account was, the sort of house I lived in, or the kind of car I drove. But the world may be different because I was important in the life of a child.

—A Teacher's Creed

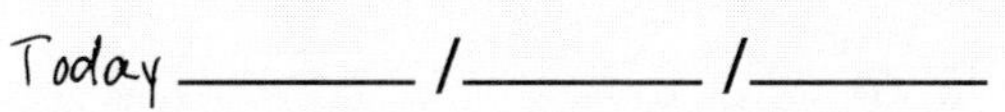

God's Words for Me Today: Direct Your Hearts

May the Lord direct your hearts into the love of God and into the steadfastness and patience of Christ.

2 Thessalonians 3:5

Today's most important things to do:

1. ______________________________
2. ______________________________
3. ______________________________
4. ______________________________
5. ______________________________
6. ______________________________

I am grateful for ______________________________

Today, my goal is ______________________________

Today, I will ______________________________

Today, I feel ______________________________

Today's Positive Thought

Go confidently in the direction of your dreams. Live the life you have imagined.

—Henry David Thoreau

Today ______ /______ /______

God's Words for Me Today: Your Strength

Look well to yourself to your own personality and to your teaching; persevere in these things for by so doing you will save both yourself and those who hear you.

1 Timothy 4:16

Today's most important things to do:

1. ______________________________
2. ______________________________
3. ______________________________
4. ______________________________
5. ______________________________
6. ______________________________

I am grateful for ______________________________

____

____

____

Today, my goal is ______________________________

____

____

____

Today, I will ______________________________

____

____

Today, I feel ____________________

____

____

____

Today's Positive Thought

The best test in life is obedience.

—Thomas S. Monson

Today ______ /______ /______

God's Words for Me Today: Spiritual Maturity

Let us go on and get past the elementary stage in the teachings and doctrine of Christ, advancing steadily toward the completeness that belongs to spiritual maturity.

Hebrews 6:1

Today's most important things to do:

1. ____________________
2. ____________________
3. ____________________
4. ____________________
5. ____________________
6. ____________________

I am grateful for ____________________

____

____

____

Today, my goal is ____

____

____

____

Today, I will ____

____

____

Today, I feel ____

____

____

____

Today's Positive Thought

Today I will think on childhood memories. I will remember the wonder of snapdragons in our garden. Did you ever squeeze a snapdragon's jaws and watch the mouth open?

—Valerie Hill

Today ________ /________ /________

God's Words for Me Today: He Leads Me

He refreshes and restores my life; he leads me in the paths of righteousness for his names sake, he prepares a table before me; my cup runs over.

Psalm 23:4–5

Today's most important things to do:

1. ________________________________
2. ________________________________
3. ________________________________

4. ______________________________

5. ______________________________

6. ______________________________

I am grateful for ______________________________

____

____

____

Today, my goal is ______________________________

____

____

____

Today, I will ______________________________

____

____

Today, I feel ______________________________

____

____

____

Today's Positive Thought

One must have sunshine, freedom, and a little flower.

—Hans Christian Andersen

Today ________ /________ /________

God's Words for Me Today: Guard Your Heart

> And the peace of God, which transcends all understanding, will guard your hearts and your minds in Christ Jesus.
>
> Philippians 4:7

Today's most important things to do:

1. ________________________________
2. ________________________________
3. ________________________________
4. ________________________________
5. ________________________________
6. ________________________________

I am grateful for ________________________________

____

____

____

Today, my goal is ________________________________

____

____

____

Today, I will ________________________________

____

____

Today, I feel ________________________________

____

____

____

Today's Positive Thought

Herbs growing in my garden brighten my day! They encourage me to spice up my cooking, enjoy the scents and relish in the joy of the life of a garden.

—Valerie Hill

Today ______ /______ /______

God's Words for Me Today: His Light Comes through Me

Who came as a witness to the light so that through him men might believe?

John 1:7

Today's most important things to do:

1. ______________________
2. ______________________
3. ______________________
4. ______________________
5. ______________________
6. ______________________

I am grateful for ______________________

____

____

____

Today, my goal is ______________________

____

Today, I will

Today, I feel

Today's Positive Thought

There is more to life than increasing its speed.

—Gandhi

Today ______ /______ /______

God's Words for Me Today: Delight in His Beauty

In his hands are the depths of the earth, and the tops of the mountains are his. His is the sea, for he has made it, and the dry land, which his hands have formed.

Psalm 95:4–5

Today's most important things to do:

1. ______
2. ______
3. ______
4. ______

5. ____________________________________

6. ____________________________________

I am grateful for ____________________________________

____

____

____

Today, my goal is ____________________________________

____

____

____

Today, I will ____________________________________

____

____

Today, I feel ____________________________________

____

____

____

Today's Positive Thought

There's absolutely no reason for being rushed along with the rush. Everybody should be free to go very slow.

—Robert Frost

Today ______ / ______ / ______

God's Words for Me Today: Ask Jesus

Anything you ask me in my name I will do.

John 14:14

Today's most important things to do:

1. ____________________
2. ____________________
3. ____________________
4. ____________________
5. ____________________
6. ____________________

I am grateful for ____________________

Today, my goal is ____________________

Today, I will ____________________

Today, I feel ____________________

Today's Positive Thought

The nutritionists are ruining our food.

—Julia Child

Today ______ / ______ / ______

God's Words for Me Today: Jesus Loves Me

As the father has loved me, so I have loved you. Live on in my love.

John 15:9

Today's most important things to do:

1. ________________________________
2. ________________________________
3. ________________________________
4. ________________________________
5. ________________________________
6. ________________________________

I am grateful for ________________________________

____

____

____

Today, my goal is ________________________________

____

____

____

Today, I will ________________________________

____

____

Today, I feel ________________________________

____

Today's Positive Thought

Life itself is the proper binge.

—Julia Child

Today ______ /______ /______

God's Words for Me Today: Jesus Is the Light of the World

The people who walked in darkness have seen a great light.

Isaiah 9:2

Today's most important things to do:

1. ______
2. ______
3. ______
4. ______
5. ______
6. ______

I am grateful for ______

Today, my goal is ______

____

____

Today, I will ______________________________________

____

____

Today, I feel ______________________________________

____

____

____

Today's Positive Thought

How I wish that somewhere there existed an island for those that are wise and of good will.

—Albert Einstein

Today _______ /_______ /_______

God's Words for Me Today: He Sent His Spirit

I will ask the father, and he will give you another comforter that he may remain with you forever.

John 14:16

Today's most important things to do:

1. ______________________________
2. ______________________________
3. ______________________________
4. ______________________________

5. ______________________________________

6. ______________________________________

I am grateful for ______________________________________

____

____

____

Today, my goal is ______________________________________

____

____

____

Today, I will ______________________________________

____

____

Today, I feel ______________________________________

____

____

____

Today's Positive Thought

Earth laughs in flowers.

—Ralph Waldo Emerson

Today ______ /______ /______

God's Words for Me Today: Be Still and Rest in Jesus

Return to your rest, O my soul, for the lord has dealt bountifully with you.

Psalm 116:6–7

Today's most important things to do:

1. ______
2. ______
3. ______
4. ______
5. ______
6. ______

I am grateful for ______

______

______

______

Today, my goal is ______

______

______

______

Today, I will ______

______

______

Toc :el ___

Today's Positive Thought

It is perhaps a more fortunate destiny to have a taste for collecting shells than to be born a millionaire.

—Robert Louis Stevenson

Today ___ / ___ / ___

God's Words for Me Today: Amen—So It Is

The time is fulfilled, and the kingdom of God is at hand.

Mark 1:15

Today's most important things to do:

1. ___
2. ___
3. ___
4. ___
5. ___
6. ___

I am grateful for ___

Today, my goal is ____________________

____

____

____

Today, I will ____________________

____

____

Today, I feel ____________________

____

____

____

Today's Positive Thought

The highlight of my childhood was making my brother laugh so hard that food came out his nose.

—Garrison Keillor

Today _______ /_______ /_______

God's Words for Me Today: Jesus Cares

In him my heart trusts, and I am helped.

Psalm 28:7

Today's most important things to do:

1. ____________________
2. ____________________
3. ____________________
4. ____________________

5. ______________________________

6. ______________________________

I am grateful for ______________________________

____

____

____

Today, my goal is ______________________________

____

____

____

Today, I will ______________________________

____

____

Today, I feel ______________________________

____

____

____

Today's Positive Thought

Long live the sun which gives us such color.

—Paul Cezanne

Today _______ / _______ / _______

God's Words for Me Today: Jesus Is a Light unto My Feet

I am the light of the world. He who follows me will not be walking in the dark, but will have the light which is life.

John 8:12

Today's most important things to do:

1. ______________________________
2. ______________________________
3. ______________________________
4. ______________________________
5. ______________________________
6. ______________________________

I am grateful for ______________________________

____

____

____

Today, my goal is ______________________________

____

____

____

Today, I will ______________________________

____

____

Today, I feel ____

____

____

____

Today's Positive Thought

Oh, for a book and a shady nook, either in door or out.

—John Wilson

Today ________ /________ /________

God's Words for Me Today: Love One Another

Love one another. Just as I have loved you.

John13:34

Today's most important things to do:

1. ________________________________
2. ________________________________
3. ________________________________
4. ________________________________
5. ________________________________
6. ________________________________

I am grateful for ____

____

____

____

Today, my goal is ____

____

Today, I will

Today, I feel

Today's Positive Thought

Housework when done correctly can kill you.

—Author Unknown

Today ______ / ______ / ______

God's Words for Me Today: My Being Glorifies His Name

When you bear much fruit, my father is honored and glorified.

John 15:8

Today's most important things to do:

1.
2.
3.
4.
5.
6.

I am grateful for ______________________________

____

____

____

Today, my goal is ______________________________

____

____

____

Today, I will ______________________________

____

____

Today, I feel ______________________________

____

____

____

Today's Positive Thought

Woe to the cook whose sauce has no sting.

—Chaucer

Today ________ /________ /________

God's Words for Me Today: His Name

For to us a child is born to us a son is given; and the government shall be upon his shoulder, and his name shall be called wonderful counselor.

Isaiah 9:6

Today's most important things to do:

1. ______________________________
2. ______________________________
3. ______________________________
4. ______________________________
5. ______________________________
6. ______________________________

I am grateful for ______________________________

____

____

____

Today, my goal is ______________________________

____

____

____

Today, I will ______________________________

____

____

Today, I feel ______________________________

____

____

____

Today's Positive Thought

God has given us our memories that we might have roses in December.

—J. M. Barrie

Today ______ /______ /______

God's Words for Me Today: Pray Often

I am telling you, whatever you ask for in prayer, believe that it is granted to you.

Mark 11:24

Today's most important things to do:

1. ______
2. ______
3. ______
4. ______
5. ______
6. ______

I am grateful for ______

______

______

______

Today, my goal is ______

______

______

______

Today, I will ______

______

______

Today, I feel ______

______

Today's Positive Thought

Manners are a sensitive awareness of the feeling of others. If you have that awareness, you have good manners, no matter what fork you use.

—Emily Post

God's Words for Me Today: Be Grateful to Jesus

That I may make the voice of thanksgiving heard and may tell of all your wondrous works.

Psalm 26:7

Today's most important things to do:

1. __________
2. __________
3. __________
4. __________
5. __________
6. __________

I am grateful for __________

Today, my goal is __________

Today, I will ___

Today, I feel ___

Today's Positive Thought

I expand and live in the warm day like corn and melons.

—Ralph Waldo Emerson

Today ___ /___ /___

God's Words for Me Today: Jesus Is Good

Taste and see that the lord is good! Blessed is the man who trusts and takes refuge in him.

Psalm 34:8

Today's most important things to do:

1. ___
2. ___
3. ___
4. ___
5. ___
6. ___

I am grateful for ___

Today, my goal is ______

Today, I will ______

Today, I feel ______

Today's Positive Thought

When one has tasted watermelon he knows what the angels eat.

—Mark Twain

Today ______ / ______ / ______

God's Words for Me Today: Jesus Instructs

The Lord will instruct you and teach you in the way you should go; I will counsel you with my eye upon you.

Psalm 32:8

Today's most important things to do:

1. ______
2. ______
3. ______

4. ______________________________________

5. ______________________________________

6. ______________________________________

I am grateful for ______________________________________

____

____

____

Today, my goal is ______________________________________

____

____

____

Today, I will ______________________________________

____

____

Today, I feel ______________________________________

____

____

____

Today's Positive Thought

Women sit or move to and fro, some old, some young. The young are beautiful but the old are more beautiful than the young.

—Walt Whitman

Today ______ /______ /______

God's Words for Me Today: Come Home to Jesus

You will show me the path to life, in your presence, is fullness of joy, at your right hand there are pleasures forevermore.

Psalm 16:11

Today's most important things to do:

1. ______________________________
2. ______________________________
3. ______________________________
4. ______________________________
5. ______________________________
6. ______________________________

I am grateful for ______________________________

____

____

____

Today, my goal is ______________________________

____

____

____

Today, I will ______________________________

____

____

Today, I feel ______________________________

____

____

____

Today's Positive Thought

Charm: the quality in others that makes us more satisfied with ourselves.

—Henri-Frederik Amiel

Today ______ /______ /______

God's Words for Me Today: See Jesus Today

I assure you, as often as you did it for one of the least of my brethren, you did it for me.

Matthew 25:40

Today's most important things to do:

1. ______________________________
2. ______________________________
3. ______________________________
4. ______________________________
5. ______________________________
6. ______________________________

I am grateful for ______________________________

____

____

____

Today, my goal is ______________________________

____

____

____

Today, I will ______________________________

____

____

Today, I feel ______________________________

____

____

____

Today's Positive Thought

Health is the thing that makes you feel like now is the best time of the year.

—Franklin Pierce Adams

Today ______ /______ /______

God's Words for Me Today: Jesus Delights in Me

Behold my servant. My elect in whom my soul delights.

Isaiah 42:1

Today's most important things to do:

1. ______________________________
2. ______________________________
3. ______________________________
4. ______________________________

5. ______________________________

6. ______________________________

I am grateful for ______________________________

____

____

____

Today, my goal is ______________________________

____

____

____

Today, I will ______________________________

____

____

Today, I feel ______________________________

____

____

____

Today's Positive Thought

Food is not about impressing people. It's about making them feel comfortable.

—Author unknown

Today ______ / ______ / ______

God's Words for Me Today: Jesus Plans for You

> In my father's house there are many dwelling places. I am going away to prepare a place for you.
>
> John 14:2–3

Today's most important things to do:

1. ______________________________
2. ______________________________
3. ______________________________
4. ______________________________
5. ______________________________
6. ______________________________

I am grateful for ______________________________

____

____

____

Today, my goal is ______________________________

____

____

____

Today, I will ______________________________

____

____

Today, I feel ____

____

____

____

Today's Positive Thought

Reading makes a man full.

—Francis Bacon

Today ______ / ______ / ______

God's Words for Me Today: Your Yes to Jesus

For he asked life of you and you gave it to him.

Psalms 21:4

Today's most important things to do:

1. ______________________________
2. ______________________________
3. ______________________________
4. ______________________________
5. ______________________________
6. ______________________________

I am grateful for ____

____

____

____

Today, my goal is ______________________________

____

____

____

Today, I will ______________________________

____

____

Today, I feel ______________________________

____

____

____

Today's Positive Thought

A child's life is like a piece of paper on which every person leaves a mark.

—Chinese proverb

Today _______ /_______ /_______

God's Words for Me Today: Love the Lord

Therefore you shall love the Lord your God with all your heart, with all your soul, and with all your mind, and with all your strength.

Mark 12:30

Today's most important things to do:

1. ______________________________
2. ______________________________
3. ______________________________
4. ______________________________

5. ______________________________

6. ______________________________

I am grateful for ______________________________

____

____

____

Today, my goal is ______________________________

____

____

____

Today, I will ______________________________

____

____

Today, I feel ______________________________

____

____

____

Today's Positive Thought

Being good is its own reward.

—Suzanne Schwendiman

Today _____ / _____ / _____

God's Words for Me Today: He Is the Path unto My Feet

He makes my feet like hinds feet and sets me securely upon my high places.

Psalm 18:33

Today's most important things to do:

1. ______________________
2. ______________________
3. ______________________
4. ______________________
5. ______________________
6. ______________________

I am grateful for ______________________

____

____

____

Today, my goal is ______________________

____

____

____

Today, I will ______________________

____

____

Today, I feel ____

____

____

____

Today's Positive Thought

Different people get different things at different times.

—Author Unknown

Today ______ /______ /______

God's Words for Me Today: Jesus Is Gentle

Man of God aim at righteousness, godliness, faith, love, steadfastness, and a gentleness of heart.

1 Timothy 6:11

Today's most important things to do:

1. ______________________________
2. ______________________________
3. ______________________________
4. ______________________________
5. ______________________________
6. ______________________________

I am grateful for ____

____

____

____

Today, my goal is ________________________________

____

____

____

Today, I will ________________________________

____

____

Today, I feel ________________________________

____

____

____

Today's Positive Thought

An investment in knowledge pays the best interest.

—Ben Franklin

Today ______ /______ /______

God's Words for Me Today: I Rest in Jesus

Release and you will be acquitted and forgiven.

Luke 6:37

Today's most important things to do:

1. ________________________________
2. ________________________________
3. ________________________________
4. ________________________________
5. ________________________________
6. ________________________________

I am grateful for ________________________________

____

____

____

Today, my goal is ________________________________

____

____

____

Today, I will ________________________________

____

____

Today, I feel ________________________________

____

____

____

Today's Positive Thought

The highest point of achievement yesterday is the starting point of today.

—Motto of Paulist Fathers

Today ______ /______ /______

God's Words for Me Today: Jesus Redeems

I am the resurrection and the life:

John 11:25

Today's most important things to do:

1. ______________________________
2. ______________________________
3. ______________________________
4. ______________________________
5. ______________________________
6. ______________________________

I am grateful for ______________________________

____

____

____

Today, my goal is ______________________________

____

____

____

Today, I will ______________________________

____

____

Today, I feel ______________________________

____

____

____

Today's Positive Thought

What you get by achieving your goals is not as important as what you become by achieving your goals.

—Zig Ziglar

Today ______ /______ /______

God's Words for Me Today: Jesus Is Forgiveness

I am he who blots out and cancels your transgressions, for my own sake, and I will not remember your sins.

Isaiah 43:25

Today's most important things to do:

1. ______
2. ______
3. ______
4. ______
5. ______
6. ______

I am grateful for ______

______

______

______

Today, my goal is ______

______

______

______

Today, I will ______

______

______

Today, I feel ______________________________

____

____

____

Today's Positive Thought

The measure of real success is one you cannot spend, it's the way your child describes you when speaking to a friend.

—Author Unknown

Today ______ /______ /______

God's Words for Me Today: Listen to Jesus

So speak and so act as people who are to be judged under the law of liberty, the moral instruction by Christ, especially about love.

James 2:12

Today's most important things to do:

1. ______________________________
2. ______________________________
3. ______________________________
4. ______________________________
5. ______________________________
6. ______________________________

I am grateful for ______________________________

____

____

____

Today, my goal is ____

____

____

____

Today, I will ____

____

____

Today, I feel ____

____

____

____

Today's Positive Thought

There are two lasting bequests we can give our children; one is roots, the other is wings.

—Hodding Carter

Today ________ /________ /________

God's Words for Me Today: He Is the Reason

It is I, I the Lord; there is no savior but me.

Isaiah 43:11

Today's most important things to do:

1. ______________________________________
2. ______________________________________
3. ______________________________________
4. ______________________________________

5. ______________________________

6. ______________________________

I am grateful for ______________________________

____

____

____

Today, my goal is ______________________________

____

____

____

Today, I will ______________________________

____

____

Today, I feel ______________________________

____

____

____

Today's Positive Thought

Every day is a fresh start day!

—Valerie Hill

Today ______ / ______ / ______

God's Words for Me Today: Jesus Wants My Happiness

> Happy is everyone who fears, reveres, and worships the lord, who walks in his ways and lives according to his commandments.
>
> Psalm 128:1

Today's most important things to do:

1. ______________________________
2. ______________________________
3. ______________________________
4. ______________________________
5. ______________________________
6. ______________________________

I am grateful for ______________________________

____

____

____

Today, my goal is ______________________________

____

____

____

Today, I will ______________________________

____

____

Today, I feel ____

____

____

____

Today's Positive Thought

What gift has Providence bestowed on man that is so dear to him as children?

—Cicero

Today ________ /________ /________

God's Words for Me Today: His Family

Whoever does the will of God is my brother and sister and mother.

—Author unknown

Today's most important things to do:

1. ______________________________
2. ______________________________
3. ______________________________
4. ______________________________
5. ______________________________
6. ______________________________

I am grateful for ____

____

____

____

Today, my goal is ____

____

____

____

Today, I will ____

____

____

Today, I feel ____

____

____

____

Today's Positive Thought

Always fall in love with what you're asked to accept. Take what is given and make it over your way.

—Robert Frost

Today ________ /________ /________

God's Words for Me Today: God's Glory

Behold, even the moon has no brightness compared to God's glory.

Psalm 25:5

Today's most important things to do:

1. ________________________________
2. ________________________________
3. ________________________________
4. ________________________________

5. ____

6. ____

I am grateful for ____

____

____

____

Today, my goal is ____

____

____

____

Today, I will ____

____

____

Today, I feel ____

____

____

____

Today's Positive Thought

Acceptance, "and that's the way it is."

—Walter Cronkite

Today _______ /_______ /_______

God's Words for Me Today: Oh, Merciful Jesus

Have mercy on me, O God, in your goodness; in the greatness of your compassion wipe out my offense.

Psalm 51:3

Today's most important things to do:

1. ______________________________
2. ______________________________
3. ______________________________
4. ______________________________
5. ______________________________
6. ______________________________

I am grateful for ______________________________

____

____

____

Today, my goal is ______________________________

____

____

____

Today, I will ______________________________

____

____

Today, I feel ______________________________

____

____

____

Today's Positive Thought

Do you carrot all for me? My heart beets for you. If we cantaloupe lettuce marry; we'd make a swell pear.

—Author Unknown

Today ______ /______ /______

God's Words for Me Today: Jesus Supplies Abundantly

My God will supply your needs fully in a way worthy of his magnificent riches in Christ Jesus.

Philippians 4:19

Today's most important things to do:

1. ______________________________
2. ______________________________
3. ______________________________
4. ______________________________
5. ______________________________
6. ______________________________

I am grateful for ______________________________

____

____

____

Today, my goal is ____

____

____

____

Today, I will ____

____

____

Today, I feel ____

____

____

____

Today's Positive Thought

You gain strength, courage and confidence by every experience in which you really stop to look fear in the face.

—Eleanor Roosevelt

Today ________ /________ /________

God's Words for Me Today: Be of Love

If you keep my commandments you will abide in my love and live on in it, just as I have obeyed my father's commandments and live on in his love.

John15:10

Today's most important things to do:

1. ______________________________
2. ______________________________
3. ______________________________
4. ______________________________

5. ______________________________

6. ______________________________

I am grateful for ______________________________

____

____

____

Today, my goal is ______________________________

____

____

____

Today, I will ______________________________

____

____

Today, I feel ______________________________

____

____

____

Today's Positive Thought

A happy and gracious flexibility, lucidity of thought, freedom from prejudice and freedom from stiffness, openness of mind.

—Jean Ed LaFontaine

Today ______ /______ /______

God's Words for Me Today: The Spirit

The Lord is the spirit, and where the spirit is the Lord is, there is liberty.

2 Corinthians 3:17

Today's most important things to do:

1. ______
2. ______
3. ______
4. ______
5. ______
6. ______

I am grateful for ______

______

______

______

Today, my goal is ______

______

______

______

Today, I will ______

______

______

Today, I feel ______

______

Today's Positive Thought

The art of being wise is the art of knowing what to overlook.

—William James

Today ______ / ______ / ______

God's Words for Me Today: A Part of Jesus

> And all of us who continued to behold as in a mirror the glory of the lord, are constantly being transfigured into his very own image in ever increasing splendor and from one degree of glory to another from the lord in the spirit.
>
> 2 Corinthians 3:18

Today's most important things to do:

1. ________________________________
2. ________________________________
3. ________________________________
4. ________________________________
5. ________________________________
6. ________________________________

I am grateful for ________________________________

Today, my goal is ________________________________

____

____

Today, I will ____________________________________

____

____

Today, I feel ____________________________________

____

____

____

Today's Positive Thought

People are lonely because they build walls instead of bridges.

—Joseph Fort Newton

Today ______ / ______ / ______

God's Words for Me Today: Keep It Simple—Trust Jesus

Trust in the Lord, and do good: so shall you dwell in the land, and feed on his faithfulness, and truly you shall be fed.

Psalm 37:3

Today's most important things to do:

1. ____________________________
2. ____________________________
3. ____________________________
4. ____________________________
5. ____________________________
6. ____________________________

I am grateful for ____________________

____

____

____

Today, my goal is ____________________

____

____

____

Today, I will ____________________

____

____

Today, I feel ____________________

____

____

____

Today's Positive Thought

The strongest of all warriors are these two, Time and Patience.

—Leo Nikolaevich Tolstoi

Today ______ / ______ / ______

God's Words for Me Today: Praise Jesus

Give to the Lord, you sons of God, give to the Lord glory and praise.

Psalm 29:1

Today's most important things to do:

1. ____________________
2. ____________________
3. ____________________
4. ____________________
5. ____________________
6. ____________________

I am grateful for ____________________

Today, my goal is ____________________

Today, I will ____________________

Today, I feel ____________________

Today's Positive Thought

Peace, it is found in prayerful pondering the scriptures, observing the beauty of nature, contemplating the ocean with a 180 degree view, just sitting in one's own backyard enjoying the sunshine and watching the hummingbirds with a little pet on your lap.

—Valerie Hill

Today ______ /______ /______

God's Words for Me Today: Jesus's Strength Abides in Me

I am honorable in the eyes of the Lord and my God has become my strength.

Isaiah 49:5

Today's most important things to do:

1. ______________________
2. ______________________
3. ______________________
4. ______________________
5. ______________________
6. ______________________

I am grateful for ______________________

____

____

____

Today, my goal is ______________________

____

____

____

Today, I will ______________________

____

____

Today, I feel ____________________

____

____

____

Today's Positive Thought

Let us not look back in anger or forward in fear, but around in awareness.

—James Thurber

Today ______ /______ /______

God's Words for Me Today: Jesus Is the Truth

For those who are truthful are his delights.

Proverbs 12:22

Today's most important things to do:

1. ____________________
2. ____________________
3. ____________________
4. ____________________
5. ____________________
6. ____________________

I am grateful for ____________________

____

____

____

Today, my goal is ______________________________

____

____

____

Today, I will ______________________________

____

____

Today, I feel ______________________________

____

____

____

Today's Positive Thought

The deepest feeling always shows itself in silence.

—Marianne Moore

Today ______ /______ /______

God's Words for Me Today: Jesus Loves the Child

Allow the little ones to come to me the kingdom of God belongs to such as these.

Matthew 19:14

Today's most important things to do:

1. ______________________________
2. ______________________________
3. ______________________________
4. ______________________________

5. ______________________________

6. ______________________________

I am grateful for ______________________________

____

____

____

Today, my goal is ______________________________

____

____

____

Today, I will ______________________________

____

____

Today, I feel ______________________________

____

____

____

Today's Positive Thought

When you feel you are alone remember there are angels whose sole purpose is to embrace the lonely.

—Corrine De Winter

Today ______ /______ /______

God's Words for Me Today: Come Let Us Adore Him

Give to the Lord the glory due his name; worship the Lord in holiness.

Psalm 29:2

Today's most important things to do:

1. ________________________________
2. ________________________________
3. ________________________________
4. ________________________________
5. ________________________________
6. ________________________________

I am grateful for ________________________________

____

____

____

Today, my goal is ________________________________

____

____

____

Today, I will ________________________________

____

____

Today, I feel ____

____

____

____

Today's Positive Thought

I have lost nothing in my life that I could not find again with God.

—Corrine De Winter

Today ______ /______ /______

God's Words for Me Today: Hallelujah

This is the day the Lord has made; let us be glad and rejoice in it.

Psalm 118:24

Today's most important things to do:

1. ______________________________
2. ______________________________
3. ______________________________
4. ______________________________
5. ______________________________
6. ______________________________

I am grateful for ____

____

____

____

Today, my goal is ______________________________

____

____

____

Today, I will ______________________________

____

____

Today, I feel ______________________________

____

____

____

Today's Positive Thought

I am not afraid of storms, for I am learning how to sail my ship.

—Louisa May Alcott

Today ______ / ______ / ______

God's Words for Me Today: Jesus Is My Shepherd

Lead me in the path of your commandments, for in it I delight.

Psalm 119:35

Today's most important things to do:

1. ______________________________
2. ______________________________
3. ______________________________
4. ______________________________

5. ______________________________

6. ______________________________

I am grateful for ______________________________

____

____

____

Today, my goal is ______________________________

____

____

____

Today, I will ______________________________

____

____

Today, I feel ______________________________

____

____

____

Today's Positive Thought

Imagine not that life is all doing. Stillness, too, is life; and in that stillness the mind cluttered with busyness quiets, the heart reaching to win rests, and we hear the whispered truths of God.

—Rabbi Rami M. Shapiro

Today _______ / _______ / _______

God's Words for Me Today: I Am Safe unto the Lord

I saw the Lord ever before me for he is at my right hand that I may not be overthrown or cast down.

Acts 2:25–26

Today's most important things to do:

1. ______________________________
2. ______________________________
3. ______________________________
4. ______________________________
5. ______________________________
6. ______________________________

I am grateful for ______________________________

____

____

____

Today, my goal is ______________________________

____

____

____

Today, I will ______________________________

____

____

Today, I feel ______________________________

____

____

____

Today's Positive Thought

The wisest people are those who, although unrelenting in their quest for answers, trustingly leave some of the problems in the hands of God who knows the whole.

Rev. Dale E. Turner

Today ______ / ______ / ______

God's Words for Me Today: To Do Your Will Is My Delight

I am not seeking my own will, but the will of him who sent me.

John 5:30

Today's most important things to do:

1. ______________________________
2. ______________________________
3. ______________________________
4. ______________________________
5. ______________________________
6. ______________________________

I am grateful for ______________________________

____

____

____

Today, my goal is ______________________________

____

____

____

Today, I will ______________________________

____

____

Today, I feel ______________________________

____

____

____

Today's Positive Thought

By nature we feel hope when tragedy occurs. Hope is our instinct. Embrace it.

—Thomas C. Jordan

Today ______ /______ /______

God's Words for Me Today: Blessed

And all nations shall call you happy and blessed, for you shall be a land of delight, says the lord of hosts.

Malachi 3:12

Today's most important things to do:

1. ______________________________
2. ______________________________
3. ______________________________
4. ______________________________

5. ______________________________

6. ______________________________

I am grateful for ______________________________

____

____

____

Today, my goal is ______________________________

____

____

____

Today, I will ______________________________

____

____

Today, I feel ______________________________

____

____

____

Today's Positive Thought

Good will prevail peace will come open your heart and welcome them.

—Arlene Gay Levine

Today ______ /______ /______

God's Words for Me Today: Jesus Is Faithful

And the Father said to him, "Son, you are always with me, and everything I have is yours."

Luke 15:31

Today's most important things to do:

1. ______
2. ______
3. ______
4. ______
5. ______
6. ______

I am grateful for ______

______

______

______

Today, my goal is ______

______

______

______

Today, I will ______

______

______

Today, I feel ____

____

____

____

Today's Positive Thought

Patience is the best remedy for every trouble.

—Plautus

Today ________ /________ /________

God's Words for Me Today: Serve God Acceptably

Wherefore we receiving a kingdom which cannot be moved, let us have grace, whereby we may serve God acceptably with reverence and godly fear.

Hebrews 12:28

Today's most important things to do:

1. ______________________________
2. ______________________________
3. ______________________________
4. ______________________________
5. ______________________________
6. ______________________________

I am grateful for ____

____

____

____

Today, my goal is ______________________________

____

____

____

Today, I will ______________________________

____

____

Today, I feel ______________________________

____

____

____

Today's Positive Thought

The most important thing in life is doing what we are doing now.

—Author unknown

Today ______ /______ /______

God's Words for Me Today: Thanks Be unto God

Thanks be unto God for his unspeakable gift.

2 Corinthians 9:15

Today's most important things to do:

1. ______________________________
2. ______________________________
3. ______________________________
4. ______________________________

5. ______________________________

6. ______________________________

I am grateful for ______________________________

____

____

____

Today, my goal is ______________________________

____

____

____

Today, I will ______________________________

____

____

Today, I feel ______________________________

____

____

____

Today's Positive Thought

I know that whatever is making me feel bad is not going to last forever unless I allow it to.

—Diana Ross

Today ______ / ______ / ______

God's Words for Me Today: Profitable Doctrine

> And from a child thou hast known the holy scriptures, which are able to make thee wise unto salvation through faith which is in Christ Jesus. All scripture is given by inspiration of God, and is profitable for doctrine, for reproof, for correction, for instruction in righteousness: That the man of God may be perfect, thoroughly furnished unto all good works.
>
> 2 Timothy 3:15–17

Today's most important things to do:

1. ____________________
2. ____________________
3. ____________________
4. ____________________
5. ____________________
6. ____________________

I am grateful for ____________________

Today, my goal is ____________________

Today, I will ______________________________

____

____

Today, I feel ______________________________

____

____

____

Today's Positive Thought

Make each new morning the opening door to a better day than the one before.

—Author Unknown

Today ______ /______ /______

God's Words for Me Today: Thanks Be unto God

Search me, O God, and know my heart; test me and know my anxious thoughts. See if there is any offensive way in me, and lead me in the way everlasting.

Psalm 139: 23-24

Today's most important things to do:

1. ______________________________
2. ______________________________
3. ______________________________
4. ______________________________
5. ______________________________
6. ______________________________

I am grateful for ____________________

____

____

____

Today, my goal is ____________________

____

____

____

Today, I will ____________________

____

____

Today, I feel ____________________

____

____

____

Today's Positive Thought

Cooking done with care is an act of love.

—Craig Claiborne

Today ______ /______ /______

God's Words for Me Today: Fear Not Nor Be Dismayed

Now to him who is able to do immeasurably more than all we ask or imagine, according to his power that is at work within us.

Ephesians 3:20

Today's most important things to do:

1. ____________________
2. ____________________
3. ____________________
4. ____________________
5. ____________________
6. ____________________

I am grateful for ____________________

Today, my goal is ____________________

Today, I will ____________________

Today, I feel ____________________

Today's Positive Thought

I find that in contemplating the natural world my pleasure is greater if there are not too many others contemplating it with me, at the same time.

—Edward Abbey, *Desert Solitaire*

Today _____ / _____ / _____

God's Words for Me Today: Things Were Written Aforetime

For whatsoever things were written aforetime were written for our learning, that we through patience and comfort of the scriptures might have hope.

Romans 15:4

Today's most important things to do:

1. ______________________
2. ______________________
3. ______________________
4. ______________________
5. ______________________
6. ______________________

I am grateful for ______________________

____

____

____

Today, my goal is ______________________

____

____

____

Today, I will ______________________

____

____

Today, I feel ____

____

____

____

Today's Positive Thought

The blessings of one mountain day whatever his fate, long life, short life, stormy or calm, he is rich forever.

—John Muir

Today ______ / ______ / ______

God's Words for Me Today: What Good Thing Shall I Do?

For what is a man profited if he should gain the whole world and lose his own soul?

Matthew 16:26

Today's most important things to do:

1. ________________________________
2. ________________________________
3. ________________________________
4. ________________________________
5. ________________________________
6. ________________________________

I am grateful for ____

____

____

____

Today, my goal is ____

____

____

____

Today, I will ____

____

____

Today, I feel ____

____

____

____

Today's Positive Thought

To be seventy years young is sometimes far more cheerful and hopeful than to be forty years old.

—Oliver Wendell Holmes

Today ________ / ________ / ________

God's Words for Me Today: The Holy Ghost

But the Comforter, which is the Holy Ghost, whom the Father will send in my name, he shall teach you all things, and bring all things to your remembrance, whatsoever I have said unto you.

John 14:26

Today's most important things to do:

1. ________________________________
2. ________________________________
3. ________________________________

4. ________________________________

5. ________________________________

6. ________________________________

I am grateful for ____

____

____

____

Today, my goal is ____

____

____

____

Today, I will ____

____

____

Today, I feel ____

____

____

____

Today's Positive Thought

Let paper remember so you can forget.

—Mamie McMcCullough

Today ______ /______ /______

God's Words for Me Today: He Is Risen

He is not here: for he is risen, as he said. Come, see the place where the Lord lay. And go quickly, and tell his disciples that he is risen from the dead; and, behold, he goeth before you into Galilee; there shall ye see him: lo, I have told you. And they departed quickly from the sepulcher with fear and great joy; and did run to bring his disciples word.

Matthew 28:6–8

Today's most important things to do:

1. ______________________________
2. ______________________________
3. ______________________________
4. ______________________________
5. ______________________________
6. ______________________________

I am grateful for ______________________________

____

____

____

Today, my goal is ______________________________

____

____

____

Today, I will ____

____

____

Today, I feel ____

____

____

____

Today's Positive Thought

Amazing how we can light tomorrow with today.

—Elizabeth Barrett Browning

Today ______ /______ /______

God's Words for Me Today: And Be Not Faithless But Believing

Then saith he to Thomas, Reach hither thy finger, and behold my hands; and reach hither thy hand, and thrust it into my side: and be not faithless, but believing. And Thomas answered and said unto him, My Lord and my God.

John 20:27–28

Today's most important things to do:

1. ______________________________
2. ______________________________
3. ______________________________
4. ______________________________
5. ______________________________
6. ______________________________

I am grateful for ____

____

____

____

Today, my goal is ____

____

____

____

Today, I will ____

____

____

Today, I feel ____

____

____

____

Today's Positive Thought

Finding 365 positive thoughts sounded like an impossibility when I first began this book one thought at a time brought me to completion of my goal. The first step, find one thought then add another.

—Valerie Hill

Today ______ / ______ / ______

God's Words for Me Today: The Son of God

Jesus said unto her, I am the resurrection, and the life: he that believeth in me, though he were dead, yet shall he live: and whosoever liveth and believeth in me shall never die. Believest thou this? She saith unto him, Yea, Lord: I believe that thou art the Christ, the Son of God, which should come into the world.

John 11:25–27

Today's most important things to do:

1. ______
2. ______
3. ______
4. ______
5. ______
6. ______

I am grateful for ______

______

______

______

Today, my goal is ______

______

______

______

Today, I will ____

____

____

Today, I feel ____

____

____

____

Today's Positive Thought

Look well into thyself; there is a source of strength which will always spring up if thou wilt always look there.

—Marcus Aurelius

Today ________ /________ /________

God's Words for Me Today: Do Whatsoever I Command You

This is my commandment, That ye love one another, as I have loved you. Greater love hath no man than this, that a man lay down his life for his friends. Ye are my friends, if ye do whatsoever I command you.

John 15:12-13

Today's most important things to do:

1. ________________________________
2. ________________________________
3. ________________________________
4. ________________________________
5. ________________________________
6. ________________________________

I am grateful for ______________________________

____

____

____

Today, my goal is ______________________________

____

____

____

Today, I will ______________________________

____

____

Today, I feel ______________________________

____

____

____

Today's Positive Thought

What lies behind us and what lies before us are tiny matters compared to what lies within us.

Ralph Waldo Emerson

Today ______ /______ /______

God's Words for Me Today: Love God

But if one loves God truly, he is known by God.

1 Corinthians 8:3

Today's most important things to do:

1. ______________________________
2. ______________________________
3. ______________________________
4. ______________________________
5. ______________________________
6. ______________________________

I am grateful for ______________________________

____

____

____

Today, my goal is ______________________________

____

____

____

Today, I will ______________________________

____

____

Today, I feel ______________________________

____

____

____

Today's Positive Thought

Learn to bend. It's better than breaking.

—Author unknown

Today ______ /______ /______

God's Words for Me Today: Turn unto the Lord

Thou shalt hearken unto the voice of the Lord thy God, to keep his commandments and his statutes which are written in this book of the law, and if thou turn unto the Lord thy God with all thine heart, and with all thy soul.

Deuteronomy 30:10

Today's most important things to do:

1. ______________________________
2. ______________________________
3. ______________________________
4. ______________________________
5. ______________________________
6. ______________________________

I am grateful for ______________________________

____

____

____

Today, my goal is ______________________________

____

____

____

Today, I will ______________________________

____

____

Today, I feel ______________________________

____

____

____

Today's Positive Thought

What new face courage puts on everything!

—Ralph Waldo Emerson

Today ______ / ______ / ______

God's Words for Me Today: A Testimony of Jesus Christ Inspires Obedience

Thou shalt keep therefore his statutes, and his commandments, which I command thee this day, that it may go well with thee, and with thy children after thee, and that thou mayest prolong thy days upon the earth, which the Lord thy God giveth thee, forever.

Deuteronomy 4:40

Today's most important things to do:

1. ______________________________
2. ______________________________
3. ______________________________
4. ______________________________
5. ______________________________
6. ______________________________

I am grateful for ____

____

____

____

Today, my goal is ____

____

____

____

Today, I will ____

____

____

Today, I feel ____

____

____

____

Today's Positive Thought

A hero is an ordinary individual who finds the strength to persevere and endure in spite of overwhelming obstacles.

—Christopher Reeve

Today ________ / ________ / ________

God's Words for Me Today: A Wise Man or a Foolish Man?

Therefore whosoever heareth these sayings of mine, and doeth them, I will liken him unto a wise man, which built his house upon a rock.

Matthew 7:24

Today's most important things to do:

1. ______________________________
2. ______________________________
3. ______________________________
4. ______________________________
5. ______________________________
6. ______________________________

I am grateful for ______________________________

____

____

____

Today, my goal is ______________________________

____

____

____

Today, I will ______________________________

____

____

Today, I feel ______________________________

____

____

____

Today's Positive Thought

My grandma told me once that happiness isn't on the road to anything. That happiness is the road.

—Bob Dylan

Today ______ /______ /______

God's Words for Me Today: Rejection of the Lord Has Consequences

And Samuel said, Hath the Lord as great delight in burnt offerings and sacrifices, as in obeying the voice of the Lord?

1 Samuel 15:22

Today's most important things to do:

1. ______
2. ______
3. ______
4. ______
5. ______
6. ______

I am grateful for ______

______

______

______

Today, my goal is ______

______

______

______

Today, I will ______

______

______

Today, I feel ____________________

____

____

____

Today's Positive Thought

There's no way around grief and loss; you can dodge all you want, but sooner or later you just have to go into it, through it and hopefully, come out the other side. The world you find there will never be the same as the world you left.

—Johnny Cash

Today ______ / ______ / ______

God's Words for Me Today: Be Firm in Christ

Now it is God who makes both us and you stand firm in Christ.

2 Corinthians 1:21

Today's most important things to do:

1. ____________________
2. ____________________
3. ____________________
4. ____________________
5. ____________________
6. ____________________

I am grateful for ____________________

____

Today, my goal is ______

Today, I will ______

Today, I feel ______

Today's Positive Thought

I am designed for accomplishment, engineered for success and endowed with the seeds of greatness!

—Author unknown

Today ______ / ______ / ______

God's Words for Me Today: Whole Duty of Man: My Father's Will

For this is my Father's will and his purpose, that everyone that sees the Son and believes in and cleaves to and trusts in and relies on Him should have eternal life, and I will raise him up at the last day.

John 6:40

Today's most important things to do:

1. ____________________
2. ____________________
3. ____________________
4. ____________________
5. ____________________
6. ____________________

I am grateful for ____________________

Today, my goal is ____________________

Today, I will ____________________

Today, I feel ____________________

Today's Positive Thought

They are able who think they are able.

—Virgil

Today ______ /______ /______

God's Words for Me Today: Acquaint

Acquaint now thyself with him, and be at peace: thereby good shall come unto thee.

Job 22:21

Today's most important things to do:

1. ______________________
2. ______________________
3. ______________________
4. ______________________
5. ______________________
6. ______________________

I am grateful for ______________________

____

____

____

Today, my goal is ______________________

____

____

____

Today, I will ______________________

____

____

Today, I feel ______________________

____

Today's Positive Thought

Fear is the dark room where negatives are developed.

—Unknown

Today ______ /______ /______

God's Words for Me Today: I Shall Not Want

The Lord is my shepherd; I shall not want.

Psalms 23:1

Today's most important things to do:

1. ______
2. ______
3. ______
4. ______
5. ______
6. ______

I am grateful for ______

Today, my goal is ______

Today, I will ____

____

____

Today, I feel ____

____

____

____

Today's Positive Thought

Definition of FEAR: False Evidence Appearing Real.

—Zig Ziglar

Today ______ /______ /______

God's Words for Me Today: Pray in Secret

But thou, when thou prayest, enter into thy closet, and when thou hast shut thy door, pray to thy Father which is in secret; and thy Father which seeth in secret shall reward thee openly.

Matthew 6:6

Today's most important things to do:

1. ______________________________
2. ______________________________
3. ______________________________
4. ______________________________
5. ______________________________
6. ______________________________

I am grateful for ____

____

Today, my goal is ______

Today, I will ______

Today, I feel ______

Today's Positive Thought

It is one of the most beautiful compensations of this life that no man can sincerely try to help another without helping himself.

—Ralph Waldo Emerson

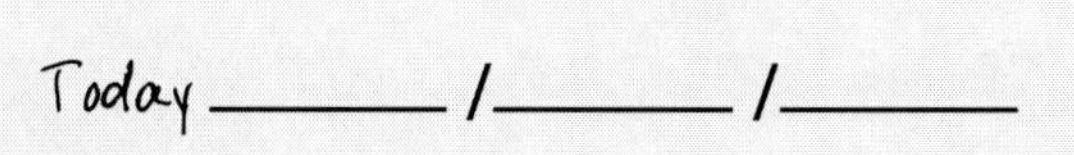

God's Words for Me Today: Pure Religion

Pure religion and undefiled before God and the Father is this, to visit the fatherless and widows in their affliction, and to keep himself unspotted from the world.

James 1:27

Today's most important things to do:

1. ______________________________
2. ______________________________
3. ______________________________
4. ______________________________
5. ______________________________
6. ______________________________

I am grateful for ______________________________

____

____

____

Today, my goal is ______________________________

____

____

____

Today, I will ______________________________

____

____

Today, I feel ______________________________

____

____

____

Today's Positive Thought

The instant you set a goal a light goes on in your future.

—Jim Paluch

Today ______ /______ /______

God's Words for Me Today: Appreciate

And Jacob loved Rachel; and said, I will serve thee seven years for Rachel thy younger daughter.

Genesis 29:18–20

Today's most important things to do:

1. ______
2. ______
3. ______
4. ______
5. ______
6. ______

I am grateful for ______

______

______

______

Today, my goal is ______

______

______

______

Today, I will ______

______

______

Today, I feel ______

______

Today's Positive Thought

There are many life lessons one can learn by knitting. A completed project begins with the first stitch.

—Valerie Hill

Today ______ /______ /______

God's Words for Me Today: Praise

Who can find a virtuous woman? For her price is far above rubies. Her children arise up, and call her blessed; her husband also, and he praiseth her.

Proverbs 31: 10-11

Today's most important things to do:

1. ______
2. ______
3. ______
4. ______
5. ______
6. ______

I am grateful for ______

Today, my goal is ______

Today, I will

Today, I feel

Today's Positive Thought

When I knit a sweater, scarf or hat for someone I think about them as I knit. It is fun to think about them wearing my gift and I wonder if they think about me when they do.

—Valerie Hill

Today ______ /______ /______

God's Words for Me Today: Believe and Prosper!

Believe in the Lord your God, so shall ye be established; believe his prophets, so shall ye prosper.

2 Chronicles 20:20

Today's most important things to do:

1. ______
2. ______
3. ______
4. ______

5. ______________________________

6. ______________________________

I am grateful for ______________________________

____

____

____

Today, my goal is ______________________________

____

____

____

Today, I will ______________________________

____

____

Today, I feel ______________________________

____

____

____

Today's Positive Thought

When I make a mistake in my knitting, I simply correct the mistake and move on.

—Valerie Hill

Today ______ / ______ / ______

God's Words for Me Today: Faint Not

And let us not be weary in well doing: for in due season we shall reap, if we faint not. As we have therefore opportunity, let us do good unto all men, especially unto them who are of the household of faith.

Galatians 6:9–10

Today's most important things to do:

1. ______
2. ______
3. ______
4. ______
5. ______
6. ______

I am grateful for ______

______

______

______

Today, my goal is ______

______

______

______

Today, I will ______

______

______

Today, I feel ____

____

____

____

Today's Positive Thought

I love to knit. My grandmother taught me how and I teach my granddaughters now, and anyone else who wants to learn as well.

—Valerie Hill

Today ______ /______ /______

God's Words for Me Today: Be Faithful

His lord said unto him, well done, thou good and faithful servant: thou hast been faithful over a few things, I will make thee ruler over many things: enter thou into the joy of thy lord.

Matthew 25:21

Today's most important things to do:

1. ______________________________
2. ______________________________
3. ______________________________
4. ______________________________
5. ______________________________
6. ______________________________

I am grateful for ____

____

Today, my goal is

Today, I will

Today, I feel

Today's Positive Thought

Be kind for everyone you know is carrying a great burden.

—Unknown author

Today ___ / ___ / ___

God's Words for Me Today: Be Converted

And said, verily I say unto you, except ye be converted, and become as little children, ye shall not enter into the kingdom of heaven.

Matthew 18:3

Today's most important things to do:

1.
2.
3.

4. ______________________________

5. ______________________________

6. ______________________________

I am grateful for ______________________________

____

____

____

Today, my goal is ______________________________

____

____

____

Today, I will ______________________________

____

____

Today, I feel ______________________________

____

____

____

Today's Positive Thought

The journey of a thousand miles begins with a single step.

—Lao-tzu

Today ______ /______ /______

God's Words for Me Today: Heirs of God

The Spirit itself beareth witness with our spirit, that we are the children of God: And if children, then heirs; heirs of God, and joint-heirs with Christ; if so be that we suffer with him, that we may be also glorified together.

Romans 8:16

Today's most important things to do:

1. ______
2. ______
3. ______
4. ______
5. ______
6. ______

I am grateful for ______

______

______

______

Today, my goal is ______

______

______

______

Today, I will ______

______

______

Today, I feel ____

____

____

____

Today's Positive Thought

When the student is ready, the teacher appears.

—Author unknown

Today ______ /______ /______

God's Words for Me Today: Know the Holy Scriptures

And that from a child thou hast known the holy scriptures, which are able to make thee wise unto salvation through faith which is in Christ Jesus.

2 Timothy 3:15

Today's most important things to do:

1. ______________________________
2. ______________________________
3. ______________________________
4. ______________________________
5. ______________________________
6. ______________________________

I am grateful for ____

____

____

____

Today, my goal is ______________________________

____

____

____

Today, I will ______________________________

____

____

Today, I feel ______________________________

____

____

____

Today's Positive Thought

Your vision will become clear only when you look into your own heart.

—Carl Jung

Today ______ /______ /______

God's Words for Me Today: Deal Truly

Lying lips are an abomination to the Lord: but they that deal truly are his delight.

Proverbs 12:22

Today's most important things to do:

1. ______________________________
2. ______________________________
3. ______________________________
4. ______________________________

5. ______________________________

6. ______________________________

I am grateful for ______________________________

____

____

____

Today, my goal is ______________________________

____

____

____

Today, I will ______________________________

____

____

Today, I feel ______________________________

____

____

____

Today's Positive Thought

Worry never robs tomorrow of its sorrow; it only saps today of its strength.

—A. J. Cronin

Today ______ /______ /______

God's Words for Me Today: Trust in the Lord!

Trust in the Lord with all thine heart; and lean not unto thine own understanding.

Proverbs 3:5

Today's most important things to do:

1. ____________________
2. ____________________
3. ____________________
4. ____________________
5. ____________________
6. ____________________

I am grateful for ____________________

____

____

____

Today, my goal is ____________________

____

____

____

Today, I will ____________________

____

____

Today, I feel ____

____

____

____

Today's Positive Thought

Nothing has changed but my attitude. Everything has changed.

—Anthony deMello

Today ______ /______ /______

God's Words for Me Today: Love One Another

A new commandment I give unto you, that ye love one another as I have loved you, that ye also love one another.

John 13:34

Today's most important things to do:

1. ______________________________
2. ______________________________
3. ______________________________
4. ______________________________
5. ______________________________
6. ______________________________

I am grateful for ____

____

____

____

Today, my goal is ____

____

____

____

Today, I will ____

____

____

Today, I feel ____

____

____

____

Today's Positive Thought

Do you want to be happy, or do you want to be right?

—Gerald Jampolsky

Today ________ /________ /________

God's Words for Me Today: Predestined

Having predestinated us unto the adoption of children by Jesus Christ to himself, according to the good pleasure of his will, to the praise of the glory of his grace, wherein he hath made us accepted in the beloved.

Ephesians 1:5

Today's most important things to do:

1. ________________________________
2. ________________________________
3. ________________________________
4. ________________________________

5. ______________________________________

6. ______________________________________

I am grateful for ____

____

____

____

Today, my goal is ____

____

____

____

Today, I will ____

____

____

Today, I feel ____

____

____

____

Today's Positive Thought

We have met the enemy and it is us.

—Walt Kelly, *Pogo*

Today _____ / _____ / _____

God's Words for Me Today: Saved Through Faith

For by grace are ye saved through faith; and that not of yourselves: it is the gift of God: not of works, lest any man should boast.

Ephesians 2:8–9

Today's most important things to do:

1. ______________________________
2. ______________________________
3. ______________________________
4. ______________________________
5. ______________________________
6. ______________________________

I am grateful for ______________________________

____

____

____

Today, my goal is ______________________________

____

____

____

Today, I will ______________________________

____

____

Today, I feel ____

____

____

____

Today's Positive Thought

O Divine Master: Grant that I may not seek so much to be loved as to LOVE.

—St. Francis of Assisi

Today ______ / ______ / ______

God's Words for Me Today: Prosper

Only be thou strong and very courageous, that thou mayest observe to do according to all the law, which Moses my servant commanded thee: turn not from it to the right hand or to the left, that thou mayest prosper whithersoever thou goest.

Joshua 1:7

Today's most important things to do:

1. ______________________________
2. ______________________________
3. ______________________________
4. ______________________________
5. ______________________________
6. ______________________________

I am grateful for ____

____

Today, my goal is ___

Today, I will ___

Today, I feel ___

Today's Positive Thought

Learn to get in touch with silence within yourself and know that everything in this life has a purpose. There are no mistakes, no coincidences, all events are blessings given to us to learn from.

—Elizabeth Kubler Ross

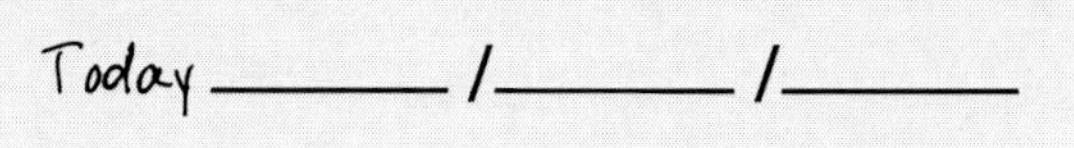

God's Words for Me Today: Rain Forty Days and Forty Nights

For yet seven days, and I will cause it to rain upon the earth forty days and forty nights; and every living substance that I have made will I destroy from off the face of the earth.

Genesis 7:4

Today's most important things to do:

1. ______________________________
2. ______________________________
3. ______________________________
4. ______________________________
5. ______________________________
6. ______________________________

I am grateful for ______________________________

____

____

____

Today, my goal is ______________________________

____

____

____

Today, I will ______________________________

____

____

Today, I feel ______________________________

____

____

____

Today's Positive Thought

Women's work is always towards wholeness.

—May Sarton

Today ______ /______ /______

God's Words for Me Today: Watch and Pray

But the end of all things is at hand: be ye therefore sober, and watch unto prayer.

1 Peter 4:7

Today's most important things to do:

1. ______________________________
2. ______________________________
3. ______________________________
4. ______________________________
5. ______________________________
6. ______________________________

I am grateful for ______________________________

____

____

____

Today, my goal is ______________________________

____

____

____

Today, I will ______________________________

____

____

Today, I feel ______________________________

____

Today's Positive Thought

How beautiful it is to do nothing and then rest afterwards.

—A Spanish proverb

Today ______ /______ /______

God's Words for Me Today: Trial

Beloved, think it not strange concerning the fiery trial which is to try you, as though some strange thing happened unto you: But rejoice, inasmuch as ye are partakers of Christ's sufferings; that, when his glory shall be revealed, ye may be glad also with exceeding joy.

1 Peter 4:12–13

Today's most important things to do:

1. ______
2. ______
3. ______
4. ______
5. ______
6. ______

I am grateful for ______

Today, my goal is ____

____

____

____

Today, I will ____

____

____

Today, I feel ____

____

____

____

Today's Positive Thought

To love oneself is the beginning of a lifelong romance.

—Oscar Wilde

Today ________ /________ /________

God's Words for Me Today: Tribulation

For verily, when we were with you, we told you before that we should suffer tribulation; even as it came to pass, and ye know.

1 Thessalonians 3:4

Today's most important things to do:

1. ______________________________
2. ______________________________
3. ______________________________
4. ______________________________

5. ________________________________

6. ________________________________

I am grateful for ________________________________

____

____

____

Today, my goal is ________________________________

____

____

____

Today, I will ________________________________

____

____

Today, I feel ________________________________

____

____

____

Today's Positive Thought

Do what you can with what you have where you are.

—Theodore Roosevelt

Today ______ /______ /______

God's Words for Me Today: We Must Learn!

But as touching brotherly love ye need not that I write unto you: for ye yourselves are taught of God to love one another.

1 Thessalonians 4:9

Today's most important things to do:

1. ___
2. ___
3. ___
4. ___
5. ___
6. ___

I am grateful for ___

Today, my goal is ___

Today, I will ___

Today, I feel ___

Today's Positive Thought

To whom much has been given, much is to be expected.

—John Kennedy

Today ______ /______ /______

God's Words for Me Today: Atonement

And not only so, but we also joy in God through our Lord Jesus Christ, by whom we have now received the atonement.

Romans 5:11

Today's most important things to do:

1. ______
2. ______
3. ______
4. ______
5. ______
6. ______

I am grateful for ______

______

______

______

Today, my goal is ______

______

______

______

Today, I will ______

______

______

Today, I feel ______

______

Today's Positive Thought

The highest form of wisdom is kindness.

—The Talmud

Today ______ /______ /______

God's Words for Me Today: Eternal Life

That as sin hath reigned unto death, even so might grace reign through righteousness unto eternal life by Jesus Christ our Lord.

Romans 5:21

Today's most important things to do:

1. ______
2. ______
3. ______
4. ______
5. ______
6. ______

I am grateful for ______

Today, my goal is ______

Today, I will

Today, I feel

Today's Positive Thought

Be the most "BRILLIANT" color in the box.

—Author Unknown

Today ______ / ______ / ______

God's Words for Me Today: Baptism

Therefore we are buried with him by baptism into death: that like as Christ was raised up from the dead by the glory of the Father, even so we also should walk in newness of life.

Romans 6:4

Today's most important things to do:

1.
2.
3.
4.
5.
6.

I am grateful for ______________________________

____

____

____

Today, my goal is ______________________________

____

____

____

Today, I will ______________________________

____

____

Today, I feel ______________________________

____

____

____

Today's Positive Thought

Recipe for a happy home: 4 cups of Love, 2 cups of Loyalty, 3 cups of Forgiveness, 1 cup of Friendship, 5 spoons of Hope, 2 spoons of Caring, 2 quarts of Truth, 1 tub of Laughter.

—Author Unknown

Today ________ /________ /________

God's Words for Me Today: Eternal Life

For the wages of sin is death; but the gift of God is eternal life through Jesus Christ our Lord.

Romans 6:23

Today's most important things to do:

1. ______________________________
2. ______________________________
3. ______________________________
4. ______________________________
5. ______________________________
6. ______________________________

I am grateful for ______________________________

Today, my goal is ______________________________

Today, I will ______________________________

Today, I feel ______________________________

Today's Positive Thought

Try a little harder to do a little better.

—Author Unknown

Today ______ /______ /______

God's Words for Me Today: Life and Peace

For to be carnally minded is death; but to be spiritually minded is life and peace.

Romans 8:6

Today's most important things to do:

1. ______
2. ______
3. ______
4. ______
5. ______
6. ______

I am grateful for ______

______

______

______

Today, my goal is ______

______

______

______

Today, I will ______

______

______

Today, I feel ______

______

____

____

Today's Positive Thought

Mis-sion-ary, {noun}: someone who leaves their family for a short time, so that others may be with their families for eternity.

—Author Unknown

Today ______ / ______ / ______

God's Words for Me Today: Walk in His Testimonies

And keep the charge of the LORD thy God, to walk in his ways, to keep his statutes, and his commandments, and his judgments, and his testimonies, as it is written in the law of Moses, that thou mayest prosper in all that thou doest, and whithersoever thou turnest thyself.

1 Kings 2:3

Today's most important things to do:

1. ______________________________
2. ______________________________
3. ______________________________
4. ______________________________
5. ______________________________
6. ______________________________

I am grateful for ______________________________

____

____

____

Today, my goal is ____

____

____

____

Today, I will ____

____

____

Today, I feel ____

____

____

____

Today's Positive Thought

Love one another, as I have loved you.

—Jesus Christ

Today _______ /_______ /_______

God's Words for Me Today: Throne of David

And King Solomon shall be blessed, and the throne of David shall be established before the LORD forever.

1 Kings 2:45

Today's most important things to do:

1. ____________________________________
2. ____________________________________
3. ____________________________________

4. ____

5. ____

6. ____

I am grateful for ____

____

____

____

Today, my goal is ____

____

____

____

Today, I will ____

____

____

Today, I feel ____

____

____

____

Today's Positive Thought

In everything give thanks.

—Author unknown

Today ______ /______ /______

God's Words for Me Today: Wisdom and Understanding

Behold, I have done according to thy words: lo, I have given thee a wise and an understanding heart; so that there was none like thee before thee, neither after thee shall any arise like unto thee.

1 Kings 3:12

Today's most important things to do:

1. ______
2. ______
3. ______
4. ______
5. ______
6. ______

I am grateful for ______

______

______

______

Today, my goal is ______

______

______

______

Today, I will ______

______

______

Today, I feel ______________________________

____

____

____

Today's Positive Thought

I loved you yesterday I love you still; I always have and I always will.

—Author Unknown

Today ______ / ______ / ______

God's Words for Me Today: Serve Others

Let him who is the greatest among you become like the youngest, and him who is the chief and leader like one who serves.

Luke 22:26

Today's most important things to do:

1. ______________________________
2. ______________________________
3. ______________________________
4. ______________________________
5. ______________________________
6. ______________________________

I am grateful for ______________________________

____

____

____

Today, my goal is ______________________________

____

____

____

Today, I will ______________________________

____

____

Today, I feel ______________________________

____

____

____

Today's Positive Thought

The future is not questionable for me it is a path of light lit by those who enrich my life.

—Johnny Cash

Today ________ /________ /________

God's Words for Me Today: Solomon's Dream

And the word of the LORD came to Solomon, and I will dwell among the children of Israel, and will not forsake my people Israel.

1 Kings 6:13

Today's most important things to do:

1. ______________________________
2. ______________________________
3. ______________________________
4. ______________________________

5. ______________________________

6. ______________________________

I am grateful for ______________________________

____

____

____

Today, my goal is ______________________________

____

____

____

Today, I will ______________________________

____

____

Today, I feel ______________________________

____

____

____

Today's Positive Thought

No act of kindness, no matter how small, is ever wasted.

—Aesop, *The Lion and the Mouse*

Today _______ /_______ /_______

God's Words for Me Today: Inseparable

Nay, in all these things we are more than conquerors through him that loved us. For I am persuaded, that neither death, nor life, nor angels, nor principalities, nor powers, nor things present, nor things to come, nor height, nor depth, nor any other creature, shall be able to separate us from the love of God, which is in Christ Jesus our Lord.

Romans 8:37–39

Today's most important things to do:

1. ______________________________
2. ______________________________
3. ______________________________
4. ______________________________
5. ______________________________
6. ______________________________

I am grateful for ______________________________

____

____

____

Today, my goal is ______________________________

____

____

____

Today, I will ____

____

____

Today, I feel ____

____

____

____

Today's Positive Thought

Diligence is the mother of good fortune.

—Cervantes

Today ______ /______ /______

God's Words for Me Today: Contentment

Not that I speak in respect of want: for I have learned, in whatsoever state I am, therewith to be content.

Philippians 4:11

Today's most important things to do:

1. ______________________________
2. ______________________________
3. ______________________________
4. ______________________________
5. ______________________________
6. ______________________________

I am grateful for ____

____

Today, my goal is

Today, I will

Today, I feel

Today's Positive Thought

All happy families are alike, but each unhappy family is unhappy in its own way.

—Leo Tolstoy

Today ______ /______ /______

God's Words for Me Today: Blessings

And I will make them and the places round about my hill a blessing; and I will cause the shower to come down in his season; there shall be showers of blessing.

Ezekiel 34:26

Today's most important things to do:

1. ______________________________
2. ______________________________
3. ______________________________
4. ______________________________
5. ______________________________
6. ______________________________

I am grateful for ______________________________

____

____

____

Today, my goal is ______________________________

____

____

____

Today, I will ______________________________

____

____

Today, I feel ______________________________

____

____

____

Today's Positive Thought

A person can be broken by too frequently bending over backwards to please others!

—Author Unknown

Today ______ /______ /______

God's Words for Me Today: Prayer

And he spake a parable unto them to this end, that men ought always to pray.

Luke 18:1

Today's most important things to do:

1. ______
2. ______
3. ______
4. ______
5. ______
6. ______

I am grateful for ______

______

______

______

Today, my goal is ______

______

______

______

Today, I will ______

______

______

Today, I feel ______

______

Today's Positive Thought

Reality. It is what it is.

—Bryan William Wayte

Today ______ / ______ / ______

God's Words for Me Today: Observe

Teaching them to observe all things whatsoever I have commanded you: and, lo, I am with you alway, even unto the end of the world. Amen.

Matthew 28:20

Today's most important things to do:

1. ______
2. ______
3. ______
4. ______
5. ______
6. ______

I am grateful for ______

Today, my goal is ______

____

____

Today, I will ____________________________________

____

____

Today, I feel ____________________________________

____

____

____

Today's Positive Thought

Saying you're sorry and showing you're sorry are not the same thing.

—Mackay

Today ______ / ______ / ______

God's Words for Me Today: Faith

Therefore I say unto you, what things so ever ye desire, when ye pray, believe that ye receive them, and ye shall have them.

Mark 11:24

Today's most important things to do:

1. ______________________________
2. ______________________________
3. ______________________________
4. ______________________________
5. ______________________________
6. ______________________________

I am grateful for ____

____

____

____

Today, my goal is ____

____

____

____

Today, I will ____

____

____

Today, I feel ____

____

____

____

Today's Positive Thought

Do for others with no desire of returned favors. We all should plant some trees we'll never sit under.

P. S. I love You by H. Jackson Brown Jr.

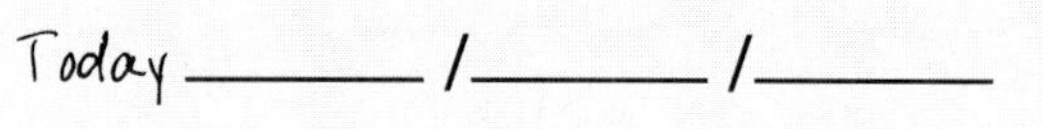

God's Words for Me Today: Patience

Rest in the Lord, and wait patiently for him,

Psalms 37:7

Today's most important things to do:

1. ______________________________

2. ______________________________

3. ______________________________

4. ______________________________

5. ______________________________

6. ______________________________

I am grateful for ______________________________

____

____

____

Today, my goal is ______________________________

____

____

____

Today, I will ______________________________

____

____

Today, I feel ______________________________

____

____

____

Today's Positive Thought

Criticize the performance—not the performer.

—Author Unknown

Today ________ /________ /________

God's Words for Me Today: Earth

Every place that the sole of your foot shall tread upon, that have I given unto you.

Joshua 1:3

Today's most important things to do:

1. ________________________________
2. ________________________________
3. ________________________________
4. ________________________________
5. ________________________________
6. ________________________________

I am grateful for ________________________________

____

____

____

Today, my goal is ________________________________

____

____

____

Today, I will ________________________________

____

____

Today, I feel ________________________________

____

___

___

Today's Positive Thought

The biggest failure of all is the person who never tries.

—Dr. Larry Kimsey

Today ______ /______ /______

God's Words for Me Today: Be Just

Now the just shall live by faith.

Hebrews 10:38

Today's most important things to do:

1. ______
2. ______
3. ______
4. ______
5. ______
6. ______

I am grateful for ______

___

___

___

Today, my goal is ______

___

___

___

Today, I will ____

____

____

Today, I feel ____

____

____

____

Today's Positive Thought

Be brilliant at the basics.

—Vince Lombardi

Today ______ /______ /______

God's Words for Me Today: He Touched Their Eyes

And when he was come into the house, the blind men came to him: and Jesus saith unto them, Believe ye that I am able to do this? They said unto him, Yea, Lord. Then touched he their eyes, saying, According to your faith be it unto you.

Matthew 9:28–29

Today's most important things to do:

1. ______________________________
2. ______________________________
3. ______________________________
4. ______________________________
5. ______________________________
6. ______________________________

I am grateful for ____

____

____

____

Today, my goal is ____

____

____

____

Today, I will ____

____

____

Today, I feel ____

____

____

____

Today's Positive Thought

A smile is the light in the window of your face that tells people that your heart is at home.

—Author Unknown

Today ________ /________ /________

God's Words for Me Today: Consider the Lilies of the Field

And why take ye thought for raiment? Consider the lilies of the field, how they grow; they toil not, neither do they spin.

Matthew 6:27

Today's most important things to do:

1. ______________________________
2. ______________________________
3. ______________________________
4. ______________________________
5. ______________________________
6. ______________________________

I am grateful for ______________________________

____

____

____

Today, my goal is ______________________________

____

____

____

Today, I will ______________________________

____

____

Today, I feel ______________________________

____

____

____

Today's Positive Thought

Take care. It is so easy to break eggs without making omelets.

—C. S. Lewis

Today ______ /______ /______

God's Words for Me Today: Clouds

If the clouds be full of rain, they empty themselves upon the earth.

Ecclesiastes 11:3

Today's most important things to do:

1. ______
2. ______
3. ______
4. ______
5. ______
6. ______

I am grateful for ______

______

______

______

Today, my goal is ______

______

______

______

Today, I will ______

______

______

Today, I feel ______

______

____

____

Today's Positive Thought

Sometimes we become so focused on the finish line, that we fail to find joy in the journey.

—Dieter F. Uchtdorf

Today ______ / ______ / ______

God's Words for Me Today: Waiting

I waited patiently for the Lord; and he inclined unto me, and heard my cry.

Psalms 40:1

Today's most important things to do:

1. ______________________________
2. ______________________________
3. ______________________________
4. ______________________________
5. ______________________________
6. ______________________________

I am grateful for ______________________________

____

____

____

Today, my goal is ______________________________

____

Today, I will ______________________________

____

____

Today, I feel ______________________________

____

____

____

Today's Positive Thought

Eighty percent of life's satisfaction comes from meaningful relationships.

—Brian Tracy

Today ______ /______ /______

God's Words for Me Today: Help

God is our refuge and strength, a very present help in trouble.

Psalms 46:1

Today's most important things to do:

1. ______________________________
2. ______________________________
3. ______________________________
4. ______________________________
5. ______________________________
6. ______________________________

I am grateful for ______________________________

____

____

____

Today, my goal is ______________________________

____

____

____

Today, I will ______________________________

____

____

Today, I feel ______________________________

____

____

____

Today's Positive Thought

Do not let the behavior of others destroy your inner peace.

—Dalai Lama

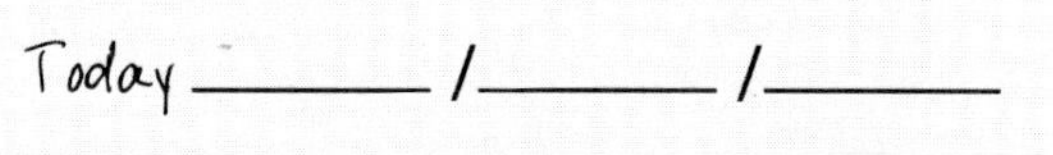

God's Words for Me Today: Vision

Where there is no vision, the people perish.

Proverbs 29:18

Today's most important things to do:

1. ______________________________
2. ______________________________
3. ______________________________
4. ______________________________
5. ______________________________
6. ______________________________

I am grateful for ______________________________

____

____

____

Today, my goal is ______________________________

____

____

____

Today, I will ______________________________

____

____

Today, I feel ______________________________

____

____

____

Today's Positive Thought

Fill your home with peace, harmony, courtesy, and love so they may be filled with the Spirit of the Lord.

—Author Unknown

Today ______ /______ /______

God's Words for Me Today: Endure Trials

> So the LORD blessed the latter end of Job more than his beginning.
>
> Job 42:12

Today's most important things to do:

1. ______
2. ______
3. ______
4. ______
5. ______
6. ______

I am grateful for ______

______

______

______

Today, my goal is ______

______

______

______

Today, I will ______

______

______

Today, I feel ______

______

____

____

Today's Positive Thought

Sympathy means I suffer with you.

—Mr. Rickie in the movie *42*

Today ______ / ______ / ______

God's Words for Me Today: Fret Not

Fret not thyself because of evildoers, neither be thou envious against the workers of iniquity.

Psalms 37:1

Today's most important things to do:

1. ____________________
2. ____________________
3. ____________________
4. ____________________
5. ____________________
6. ____________________

I am grateful for ____________________

____

____

____

Today, my goal is ____________________

____

Today, I will ___

Today, I feel ___

Today's Positive Thought

Life begins when you do.

—Mary Anne Radmacher

Today ___ / ___ / ___

God's Words for Me Today: Commandments of Men

Howbeit in vain do they worship me, teaching for doctrines the commandments of men.

Mark 7:7

Today's most important things to do:

1. ___
2. ___
3. ___
4. ___
5. ___
6. ___

I am grateful for ____

Today, my goal is ____

Today, I will ____

Today, I feel ____

Today's Positive Thought

The only thing that stands between a person and what they want from life is often the will to try it and the faith to believe it's possible.

—Rich DeVos

Today ______ /______ /______

God's Words for Me Today: Believe and Be Baptized

And as they went on their way, they came unto a certain water: and the eunuch said, See, here is water; what doth hinder me to be baptized? And Philip said, If thou believest with all thine heart, thou mayest. And he answered and said, I believe that Jesus Christ is the Son of God.

Acts 8:36–37

Today's most important things to do:

1. ______
2. ______
3. ______
4. ______
5. ______
6. ______

I am grateful for ______

______

______

______

Today, my goal is ______

______

______

______

Today, I will ____

____

____

Today, I feel ____

____

____

____

Today's Positive Thought

At 211 degrees, water is hot. At 212 degrees, it boils. And with boiling water comes steam. And steam can power a locomotive. The one extra degree... makes all the difference.

—Author Unknownv

Today ______ /______ /______

God's Words for Me Today: Filled with the Holy Ghost

And Ananias went his way, and entered into the house; and putting his hands on him said, Brother Saul, the Lord, even Jesus, that appeared unto thee in the way as thou camest, hath sent me, that thou mightest receive thy sight, and be filled with the Holy Ghost.

Acts 9:17

Today's most important things to do:

1. ______________________________
2. ______________________________
3. ______________________________
4. ______________________________

5. ________________________________

6. ________________________________

I am grateful for ____

____

____

____

Today, my goal is ____

____

____

____

Today, I will ____

____

____

Today, I feel ____

____

____

____

Today's Positive Thought

Excellence is… Caring more than others think is wise. Risking more than others think is safe. Dreaming more than others think is practical. Expecting more than others think is possible.

—Author Unknown

Today ______ /______ /______

God's Words for Me Today: The Angel of the Lord Came upon Him

And, behold, the angel of the Lord came upon him, and a light shined in the prison: and he smote Peter on the side, and raised him up, saying, Arise up quickly. And his chains fell off from his hands.

Acts 12:7

Today's most important things to do:

1. ______
2. ______
3. ______
4. ______
5. ______
6. ______

I am grateful for ______

______

______

______

Today, my goal is ______

______

______

______

Today, I will ______

______

______

Today, I feel ____

____

____

____

Today's Positive Thought

It's not the date you were born or the date that you die that matters. It's the dash in between.

—Author Unknown

Today ______ / ______ / ______

God's Words for Me Today: An Angel of the Lord Smote Him

And upon a set day Herod, arrayed in royal apparel, sat upon his throne, and made an oration unto them. And immediately the angel of the Lord smote him, because he gave not God the glory: and he was eaten of worms, and gave up the ghost. But the word of God grew and multiplied.

Acts 12:21–24

Today's most important things to do:

1. ______________________________
2. ______________________________
3. ______________________________
4. ______________________________
5. ______________________________
6. ______________________________

I am grateful for ____

____

Today, my goal is ______________________________

Today, I will ______________________________

Today, I feel ______________________________

Today's Positive Thought

Many people will walk in and out of your life, but only true friends will leave footprints on your heart.

—Eleanor Roosevelt

Today ______ /______ /______

God's Words for Me Today: Filled with Joy

For you are indeed our glory and our joy.

1 Thessalonians 2:20

Today's most important things to do:

1. ______________________________
2. ______________________________
3. ______________________________

4. ______________________________

5. ______________________________

6. ______________________________

I am grateful for ______________________________

Today, my goal is ______________________________

Today, I will ______________________________

Today, I feel ______________________________

Today's Positive Thought

The most important things in life aren't things.

—Author Unknown

Today ______ /______ /______

God's Words for Me Today: Known unto God

> Known unto God are all his works from the beginning of the world.
>
> Acts 15:18

Today's most important things to do:

1. ______________________________
2. ______________________________
3. ______________________________
4. ______________________________
5. ______________________________
6. ______________________________

I am grateful for ______________________________

____

____

____

Today, my goal is ______________________________

____

____

____

Today, I will ______________________________

____

____

Today, I feel ______________________________

____

Today's Positive Thought

N–Notice… today go about your day noticing. Take note of what you notice.

—Valerie Hill

Today ______ /______ /______

God's Words for Me Today: Saved

Thy sins are forgiven, Thy faith hath saved thee; go in peace.

Luke 7:36–50

Today's most important things to do:

1. ______
2. ______
3. ______
4. ______
5. ______
6. ______

I am grateful for ______

Today, my goal is ______

____

____

Today, I will __________________________________

____

____

Today, I feel __________________________________

____

____

____

Today's Positive Thought

B–Balance… today notice how you balance your activities. Take note of what you balance.

—Valerie Hill

Doodles and Doodads

Creativity is a spiritual action in which a person forgets about himself, moves outside himself in the creative act, absorbed by his task.

—Nikolai Berdyaev

Doodles and Doodads

Art provides a healing force which aids both the maker and the viewer.

—Richard Newman

Doodles and Doodads

To the world you may be just one person, but to one person you may be the world.

—Josephine Billings

Doodles and Doodads

Success is the side-effect of your personal dedication to a course greater than yourself.

—Earl Nightingale

Doodles and Doodads

One generation will commend your works to another; they will tell of your mighty acts.

Psalm 145:4